LEX TEMPLETON

Chenille
AMIGURUMI

21 LOW SEW & NO SEW PLUSH TOYS TO CROCHET

CONTENTS

WELCOME TO CHENILLE AMIGURUMI - 7

ABOUT THIS BOOK - 8

MATERIALS & TOOLS - 9

CROCHET TERMINOLOGY - 11

CROCHET BASICS - 11

CROCHET TECHNIQUES FOR AMIGURUMI - 13

SPECIAL STITCHES & TECHNIQUES - 14

SPECIAL TECHNIQUES - 16

NO-SEW TECHNIQUES - 19

PROJECTS

ACACIA THE BEAR - 24

MEI THE BUNNY - 30

DEBAKEY THE CAT - 36

DAISY THE DUCKLING - 44

AVRIL THE ELEPHANT - 50

FOGARTY THE FOX - 60

GARDEN FRIENDS - 68

NASH THE HEDGEHOG - 76

KORA THE KOALA - 82

ZELDA THE LLAMA - 88

ETHEL THE OSTRICH - 94

ISLA THE OTTER - 100

SAMMIE THE PANDA & BABY LOU - 106

JAKE THE PUPPY - 114

STELLA THE SHARK - 120

SATINSKY THE SWAN - 126

TEACUP BUDDIES - 132

HALLIDAY THE TIGER - 138

Acacia The Bear
P. 24

Mei the Bunny
P. 30

DeBakey the Cat
P. 36

Daisy the Duckling
P. 44

Avril the Elephant
P. 50

Fogarty The Fox
P. 60

Garden Friends
P. 68

Nash the Hedgehog
P. 76

Kora the Koala
P. 82

Zelda the Llama
P. 88

Ethel the Ostrich
P. 94

Isla the Otter
P. 100

Sammie the Panda & Baby Lou
P. 106

Jake The Puppy
P. 114

Stella The Shark
P. 120

Satinsky The Swan
P. 126

Teacup Buddies
P. 132

Halliday the Tiger
P. 138

Hello and Welcome to Chenille Amigurumi

Within this book, you will find 21 super squishy characters to crochet. Designing amigurumi has been my passion for many years now and I have slowly gravitated towards making chenille plushies. With my first solo book, I am excited to finally share these new designs and all the techniques we will use to reduce or eliminate the need for sewing. My inspiration for the book starts with my children. My youngest daughter in particular loves to play with my makes and always seems to choose the chenille toys first. In the past, I tended to switch to chenille when my hands needed a break from working with cotton, but at her request, I started to use it more and more. I am an avid craft book collector and was initially surprised at the sparsity of pattern books solely dedicated to crocheting plushies.

Chunky chenille yarn creates beautifully soft amigurumi and they work up very quickly. The popularity of this type of yarn has skyrocketed over the past few years, particularly with people who sell their makes at markets. Chenille can be a versatile fiber to work with; however, for me, the downside has always been with sewing. Shedding, snagging, and snapping (both the yarn and myself) are all common occurrences when stitching up with chenille. There are ways to make sewing pieces together easier (and we will cover these in the book); however, I have always felt that the real joy with chenille is with no-sew patterns. Following discussions with other crafters, there seemed to be an impression that making no-sew plushies meant sacrificing on design features or even individuality. With this book, I mean to convince you that neither of these is true. Another misconception is that no-sew means small or basic. Here you will find designs that vary from small to large and cater to crocheters from beginners to experienced. You may be familiar with some of the techniques used; however, I hope to surprise you with some of the construction methods I have developed on this no-sew journey.

Happy hooking and sorry for all the fluff.

Rex

ABOUT THIS BOOK

Before you pick up your hook to start, here are a few things that will help you to understand this book and the patterns within.

• All the base patterns are created using the same size yarn and hook.

To keep things as simple as possible, all the toy base patterns have been made with Hobbii yarn in one of their super chunky chenille ranges (Honey Bunny, Toucan & Baby Snuggle; 3.5 oz, 131 yds/100 g, 120 m), and a 4 mm hook.

• All the designs have been made using an X stitch single crochet.

X stitch single crochet uses a yarn under technique that will make your stitches tighter and can improve the appearance of colorwork. If you use a standard V stitch single crochet instead, the toys may be slightly larger or require more yarn than stated and colorwork may appear more slanted. Instructions for X stitch single crochet stitches may be found in the special stitches section.

• Make sure you read the orientation check points carefully.

Before key steps and attachments, you will be asked to check your position and move the start of your round if needed to ensure all the limbs and features line up correctly. Reading these sections carefully and taking your time will ensure you won't get a wonky toy or have to unravel rounds to fix things.

• What does no-sew mean?

It may surprise you that not everyone agrees on the definition of a "no-sew" pattern. 14 of the 18 patterns in this book are stated as no-sew designs. By this I mean that the base pattern and all attachments are crocheted together as you go. There will still be a yarn tail or two that will require weaving in. There are also instructions to embroider small details; however, for the majority of these the details are very small and made at a point where the inside of the head or body is easily accessible. This means, instead of embroidering them with a needle, you can use your hook to simply pull the yarn or embroidery floss through and then knot the ends together inside. There are also alternatives to embroidering small cheeks or a nose, such as blush or safety noses, if desired.

• Can I use other types of yarn to make the patterns?

Of course! The designs were made with chunky chenille in mind, but they can be made in any yarn and hook size of your choosing. Many of my amazing pattern testers made these designs using light worsted cotton or fine chenille. The end result will look a little different compared to super chunky chenille, and will be much smaller, but still very cute. I have also made some of the designs in fine chenille/velvet yarns and these yarns create beautiful pocket sized versions (just switch out your safety eyes for 6 mm ones or embroider them instead).

• Skill Levels

The majority of the patterns within this book are for crocheters working at an intermediate skill level. There are a lot of small beginner friendly no-sew plushie designs already available and I bet you will have made a few before. This book focuses on larger designs that will help you develop your no-sew skills and provide new challenges. There are also a few advanced level patterns to really get your teeth in to, such as the Elephant, Hedgehog, and Koala.

MATERIALS AND TOOLS

Hooks

To create each design I used a 4 mm hook. The only pattern that calls for an additional hook size is the Llama when making its accessories. You can of course use your favorite hook size that will complement your chosen yarn. Just be aware the quantity of yarn required may then change from that stated.

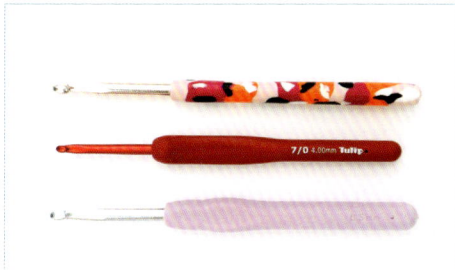

Yarn

All the yarn used within this book is from Hobbii Yarn. The two types of yarn used most in this book are Honey Bunny Chenille and Toucan Chenille. Both of these yarns are 131 yds/3.5 oz (120 m/100 g), but I would say that the Toucan chenille works up ever so slightly firmer and larger than the Honey Bunny. The colors I used are detailed in each of the patterns, but feel free to let your imagination run wild and choose any colors you like.

Safety Eyes

All the designs in this book have been made using safety eyes. I have used two different types of eyes. The more standard black eyes are 8 x 11 mm oval safety eyes that are widely available online. The larger, colorful eyes are kawaii sinker safety eyes. Plushies are the perfect makes for these sorts of eyes. There are lots of independent makers of hand-painted eyes, or you can even buy them unpainted and decorate them yourself. I have used eyes from two makers, one from the USA and one from the UK:

Darkside Crochet (UK):
http://darksidecrochet.bigcartel.com

3 J's Handcrafts (USA):
http://3jshandcrafts.com

For large sinker eyes, I recommend using a safety eye tool to insert them.

Felt Eye Alternative to Sinker Eyes

A similar effect to kawaii sinker eyes can be made using felt and a standard black safety eye. You will need a felt circle cut to the desired eye diameter and a standard circular black safety eye that is 2/3 the size of your felt disc. For example, if making a 30 mm eye, you will need to cut a 30 mm diameter circle of felt and use a 20 mm safety eye. Place the safety eye onto the felt so that it is off center and mark the position of the eye's post behind on the felt. Cut a small X in the felt and pass the post of the safety eye through. Once you have inserted the eye into your toy, the loose felt may be glued down.

Please note, safety eyes are not suitable for young children. If you intend to make your toy as a gift for a child, please refrain from using them. A safe alternative would be to embroider the eyes instead.

Toy Stuffing

Big plushies call for a lot of stuffing. Buying it in bulk can reduce your costs. I used over 70 oz (2 kg) of stuffing to create the toys in this book. I also like to bulk up my stuffing by collecting yarn ends or chenille fluff and mixing them in with the toy stuffing.

Foam Rollers

Foam rollers, like you would use to curl your hair, can be a great support to prevent a wobbly neck. The swan pattern suggests adding a foam roller to the neck to help support it. These are readily available from multiple online stockists.

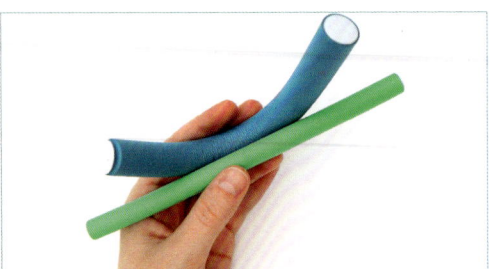

Tools

Sewing Needles:

Using big yarn often calls for big tools. When making the switch from cotton yarns I found I needed to switch over to my large stitch markers and invest in some larger needles. I still use a darning/tapestry needle for closing and weaving in yarn tails; however, for embroidery and shaping I use a doll jointing needle. These are long needles (approximately 4 inches/10 cm long) and can be ordered from online stockists.

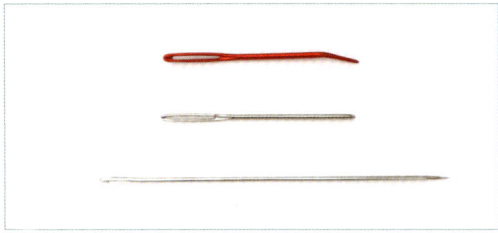

Knitting Needles:

When sewing pieces together, standard sewing pins are not strong enough to hold pieces in place as you sew. Although not required for this book, you can use knitting needles to secure pieces in place whilst they are sewn together instead of pins.

Embroidery Floss:

I like to keep facial details fairly simply, but I will often add small features using black embroidery. For plushies, I use the whole floss without separating the strands.

Blush:

Most of the designs in this book have small embroidered cheeks; however, blush is also a good alternative. I have a small compact specifically for amigurumi, but chalk or pastels also work well. Just be aware, blush will fade with time.

Crochet Terminology

This book uses US crochet terminology.

Basic Conversion Chart

US	UK
slip stitch (sl st)	slip stitch (sl st)
chain (ch)	chain (ch)
single crochet (sc)	double crochet (dc)
double crochet (dc)	treble crochet (tr)
half-double crochet (hdc)	half treble (htr)
treble (triple) crochet (tr)	double treble (dtr)

Abbreviations of the Basic Stitches

ch	Chain Stitch
sl st	Slip Stitch
sc	Single Crochet Stitch
hdc	Half-Double Crochet Stitch
dc	Double Crochet Stitch
tr	Treble (or Triple) Crochet Stitch

Concise Action Terms

dec	Decrease (reduce by one or more stitches)
inc	Increase (add one or more stitches)
join	Join two stitches together, usually with a slip stitch. (Either to complete the end of a round or when introducing a new ball or color of yarn)
rep	Repeat (the previous marked instructions)
turn	Turn your crochet piece so you can work back for the next row/round
yo	Yarn over the hook. (Either to pull up a loop or to draw through the loops on hook)

Standard Symbols Used in Patterns

[ ]	Work instructions within brackets as many times as directed
( )	Work instructions within parentheses in same stitch or space indicated
*	Repeat the instructions following the single asterisk as directed
**	1) Repeat instructions between asterisks as many times as directed; or 2) Repeat from a given set of instructions

Crochet Basics

Slip Knot

Almost every crochet project starts with a slip knot on the hook. This is not mentioned in any pattern – it is assumed.

To make a slip knot, form a loop with your yarn (the tail end hanging behind your loop); insert the hook through the loop, and pick up the ball end of the yarn. Draw yarn through loop. Keeping loop on hook, gently tug the tail end to tighten the knot. Tugging the ball end tightens the loop.

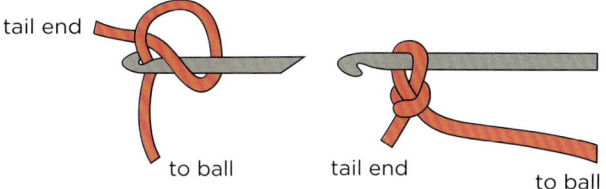

Yarn Over (yo)

This is a common practice, especially with the taller stitches. With a loop on your hook, wrap the yarn (attached to the ball) from back to front around the shaft of your hook.

Chain Stitch (ch)

The chain stitch is the foundation of most crochet projects. The foundation chain is a series of chain stitches in which you work the first row of stitches.

To make a chain stitch, you start with a slip knot (or loop) on the hook. Yarn over and pull the yarn through the loop on your hook (first chain stitch made). For more chain stitches, repeat: Yarn over, pull through loop on hook.

Hint Don't pull the stitches too tight, otherwise they will be difficult to work in. When counting chain stitches, do not count the slip knot, nor the loop on the hook. Only count the number of 'V's.

Slip Stitch (sl st)

Starting with a loop on your hook, insert hook in stitch or space specified and pull up a loop, pulling it through the loop on your hook as well.

The slip stitch is commonly used to attach new yarn and to join rounds.

Attaching a New Color or New Ball of Yarn or Joining with a Slip Stitch (join with sl st)

Make a slip knot with the new color (or yarn) and place loop on hook. Insert hook from front to back in the (usually) first stitch (unless specified otherwise). Yarn over and pull loop through stitch and loop on hook (slip stitch made).

Single Crochet (sc)

Starting with a loop on your hook, insert hook in stitch or space specified and draw up a loop (two loops on hook). Yarn over and pull yarn through both the loops on your hook (first sc made).

The height of a single crochet stitch is one chain high.

When working single crochet stitches into a foundation chain, begin the first single crochet in the second chain from the hook. The skipped chain stitch provides the height of the stitch.

At the beginning of a single crochet row or round, start by making one chain stitch (to get the height) and work the first single crochet stitch into first stitch.

Note: The one chain stitch is never counted as a single crochet stitch.

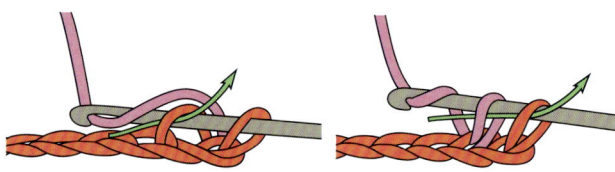

Half-Double Crochet (hdc)

Starting with a loop on your hook, yarn over hook before inserting hook in stitch or space specified and draw up a loop (three loops on hook). Yarn over and pull yarn through all three loops (first hdc made).

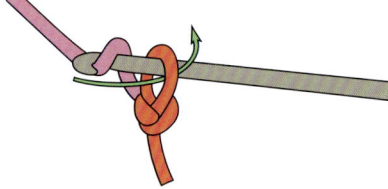

The height of a half-double crochet stitch is two chains high.

When working half-double crochet stitches into a foundation chain, begin the first stitch in the third chain from the hook. The two skipped chains provide the height. When starting a row or round with a half-double crochet stitch, make two chain stitches and work in the first stitch.

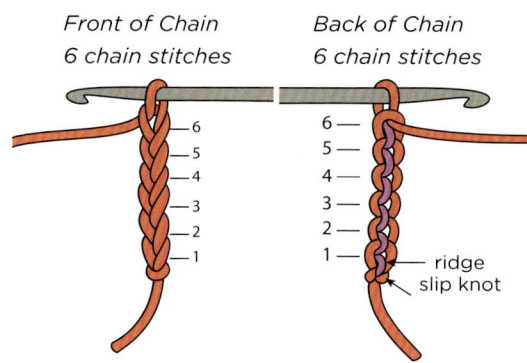

Front of Chain — 6 chain stitches
Back of Chain — 6 chain stitches
ridge
slip knot

Note: The two chain stitches are never counted as a half-double stitch.

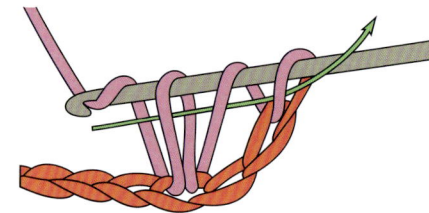

Double Crochet (dc)

Starting with a loop on your hook, yarn over hook before inserting hook in stitch or space specified and draw up a loop (three loops on hook). Yarn over and pull yarn through two loops (two loops remain on hook). Yarn over and pull yarn through remaining two loops on hook (first dc made).

The height of a double crochet stitch is three chains high. When working double crochet stitches into a foundation chain, begin the first stitch in the fourth chain from the hook.

The three skipped chains count as the first double crochet stitch. When starting a row or round with a double crochet stitch, make three chain stitches (which count as the first double crochet), skip the first stitch (under the chains) and work a double crochet in the next (second) stitch. On the following row or round, when you work in the 'made' stitch, you will be working in the top chain (3rd chain stitch of the three chains).

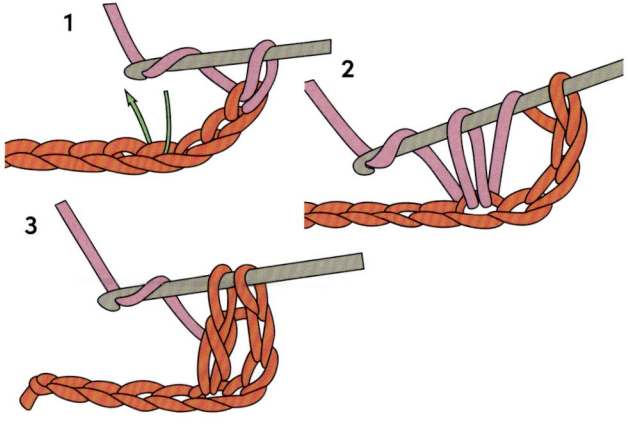

Treble (Or Triple) Crochet (tr)

Starting with a loop on your hook, yarn over hook twice before inserting hook in stitch or space specified and draw up a loop (four loops on hook). Yarn over and pull yarn through two loops (three loops remain on hook). Again, make a yarn over and pull yarn through two loops (two loops remain on hook). Once more, yarn over and pull through remaining two loops (first tr made).

The height of a treble crochet stitch is four chains high. When working treble crochet stitches into a foundation chain, begin the first stitch in the fifth chain from the hook. The four skipped chains count as the first treble crochet stitch. When starting a row or round with a treble crochet stitch, make four chain stitches (which count as the first treble crochet), skip the first stitch (under the chains) and work a treble crochet in the next (second) stitch. On the following row or round, when you work in the 'made' stitch, you will be working in the top chain (4th chain stitch of the four chains).

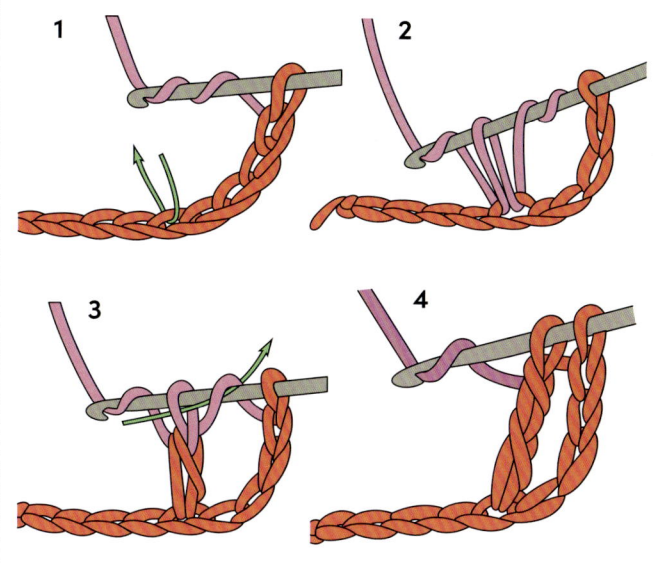

CROCHET TECHNIQUES FOR AMIGURUMI

Back Ridge Of Foundation Chain

The back ridge (also called back bumps or back bars) is found on wrong side of the foundation chain. It consists of single loops behind the 'V-loops'. To work in the back ridge, one inserts the hook from front to back through the back ridge loop to pull up the yarn. Working in the Back Ridge gives a neater finish to projects.

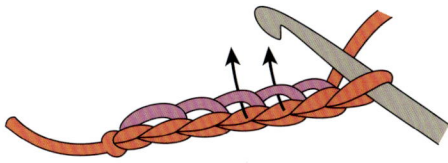

Close The Opening

Working in the stitches of the last round, insert the yarn needle from back to front through the front loop of each stitch around. Gently pull the yarn to tighten the hole. Once the opening is closed, secure the yarn. Insert the needle back through the center of the ring and taking care (squashing the stuffing), bring it out at an inconspicuous place on the piece.

Work a few weaving stitches before inserting the needle back through the stuffed piece and out at another point. Cut the yarn close to the piece so that it retracts into the stuffing.

Fasten Off

After the last single crochet stitch is worked, work a slip stitch in the next stitch. Cut the yarn, leaving a tail. With the tail, yarn over and pull the tail through the stitch.

Front And Back Loops

Every stitch has what looks like 'V's on the top. There are two loops that make up the 'V'. The front loop is the loop closest to you and the back loop is the loop furthest from you. Generally, we work in both loops – under both the front and back loops. Working in either the front or back loops only, creates a decorative ridge (made up of the unworked loops).

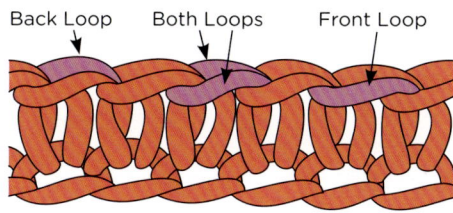

Note Work all stitches under both loops unless otherwise instructed.

Invisible Join

After the last stitch is worked (do not slip stitch in next stitch), cut the yarn leaving a tail and pull the tail through the last stitch. Using the tail and a yarn needle, skip the next stitch and insert the needle under both loops of the following stitch. Then insert the needle into the back loop of the last stitch made (the same stitch where the tail came through) and also through the horizontal loop of the stitch (for stability). Gently tug the yarn so that it looks like a "stitch" and matches the others. Secure this "stitch" and weave in the tail.

Special Stitches & Techniques

X Stitch Single Crochet (sc)

All the designs in this book have been made using the X stitch single crochet technique. This technique makes tighter stitches compared to a standard V stitch single crochet. It is particularly useful when making designs with a lot of colorwork because it makes color changes look neater.

Starting with a loop on your hook, insert hook into the stitch specified, yarn under and pull a loop through (2 loops on hook), yarn over and pull a loop through all loops on hook. *(images 1 - 6)*

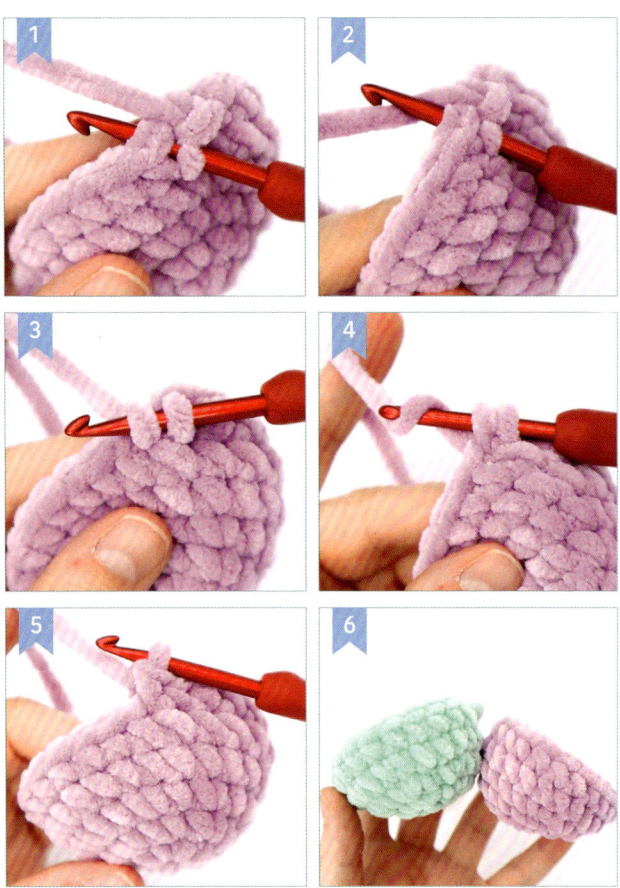

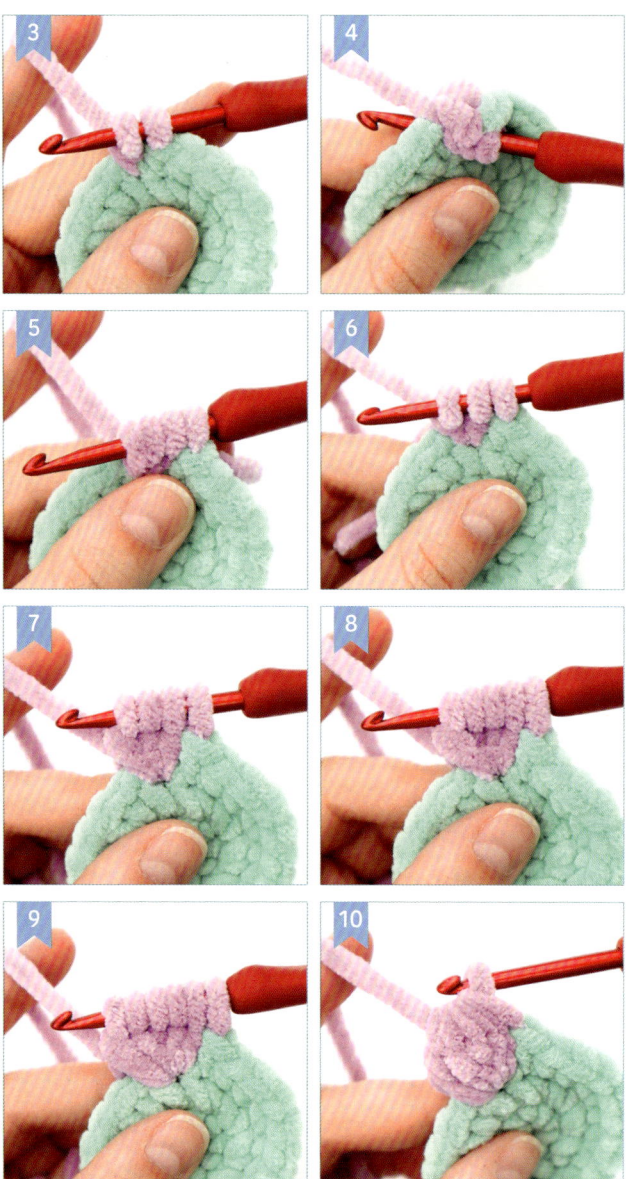

Puff Stitch (puff)

Starting with a loop on your hook, yarn over and insert hook in the next stitch. Yarn over and pull a loop through (3 loops on hook). Yarn over and pull through 2 loops on hook (2 loops remain on hook). Repeat this process into the **same stitch** 4 more times (6 loops remain on hook). Yarn over and pull through all loops on hook. *(images 1 - 10)*

½ Puff Stitch (½-puff)

Starting with a loop on your hook, yarn over and insert hook in the next stitch. Yarn over and pull a loop through (3 loops on hook). Yarn over and pull through 2 loops on hook (2 loops remain on hook). Repeat this process into the **same stitch** 1 more time (3 loops remain on hook). Yarn over and pull through all loops on hook. *(images 1 & 2)*

Loop Stitch (LoopSt)

Starting with a loop on your hook, insert hook in the next stitch. Using your index finger, pull your yarn downwards in front of your work to form a long loop. Yarn over and pull a loop through, ensuring you still have a long loop of yarn in front of your work. Yarn over and pull through both loops on hook. *(images 1-5)*

Loop Stitch Increase (LoopSt-inc)

Insert hook into the next stitch and complete the first Loop Stitch. Insert hook into the same stitch and complete the second Loop Stitch.

Loop Stitch Decrease (LoopSt-dec)

Starting with a loop on your hook, insert hook into the front loop only of each of the next 2 stitches. Using your index finger, pull your yarn downwards in front of your work to form a long loop. Yarn over and pull a loop through both of the front loops, ensuring you still have a long loop of yarn in front of your work. Yarn over and pull through both loops on hook.

Front Post Single Crochet (FPsc)

Starting with a loop on your hook, insert hook front to back through the gap on the right-hand side of the next stitch, then back to front through the gap on the left-hand side of the stitch (around the post of the stitch). Yarn over and pull a loop through (2 loops on hook). Yarn over and pull through both loops on hook.

Front Post Half Double Crochet (FPhdc)

Starting with a loop on your hook, yarn over and insert hook front to back through the gap on the right-hand side of the next stitch, then back to front through the gap on the left-hand side of the stitch (around the post of the stitch). Yarn over and pull a loop through (3 loops on hook). Yarn over and pull through all three loops on hook.

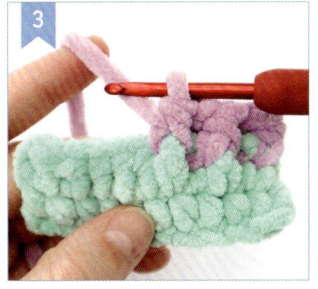 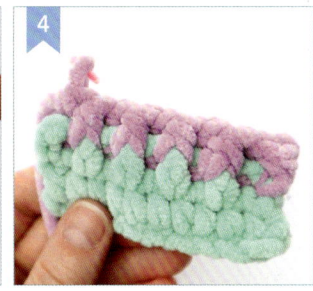

Back Post Half Double Crochet (BPhdc)

Starting with a loop on your hook, yarn over and insert hook back to front through the gap on the right-hand side of the next stitch, then front to back through the gap on the left-hand side of the stitch (around the post of the stitch). Yarn over and pull a loop through (3 loops on hook). Yarn over and pull through all three loops on hook.

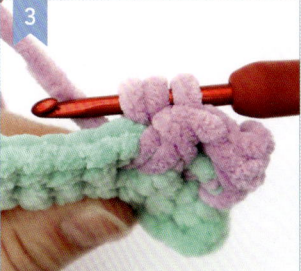 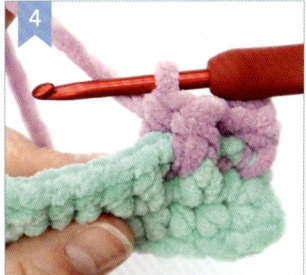

Picot Stitch (PICOT)

Starting with a loop on your hook, chain 3, then slip stitch into the 3rd chain from hook.

SPECIAL TECHNIQUES

How to Prevent Coning

Some designs within this book start with 6 single crochet stitches in a magic ring. If you find that your work becomes more of a cone than a flat circle as you continue, you may want to start with 8 single crochet stitches in the magic ring instead.

Example:

Starting with 6 sc in a magic ring	Starting with 8 sc in a magic ring alternative
1. Make a magic ring, 6 sc in ring. (6 sc)	1. Make a magic ring, 8 sc in ring. (8 sc)
2. Inc in each st around. (12 sc)	2. Inc in each st around. (16 sc)
3. [Sc in next st, inc in next st] 6 times. (18 sc)	3. [Sc in next st, inc in next st) 8 times. (24 sc)
4. [Sc in each of next 2 sts, inc in next st] 6 times. (24 sc)	

Invisible Color Changes

In order to change colors invisibly, you will need to change yarns in the stitch **before** the intended color change. Basically, the last yarn over of the stitch before the color change is made with the new color yarn. For a single crochet, you would insert you hook into the next stitch, yarn over and pull a loop through, then yarn over with the **new color** yarn and then pull through all loops on your hook. Your previous color yarn is now loose behind your stitches and the new color is on your hook. Continue in the new color and crochet over the loose end and/or knot the ends together to secure them. *(images 1 - 3)*

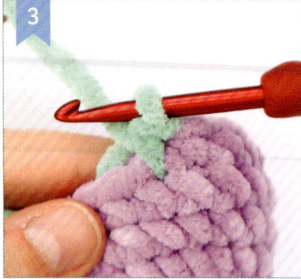

Colorwork Techniques

I recommend using an X stitch technique for your toys, particularly for any that involve colorwork. The X stitch technique provides a tighter stitch and can make your color changes look neater.

When crocheting colorwork with multiple color changes, you may choose to either cut and tie the yarn each time or carry the yarn over on the wrong side/inside of the piece.

For color changes occurring over short distances, I tend to carry the yarn over. After using the invisible color change technique, continue making stitches in the new color. Every 2 to 3 stitches, crochet over the yarn of the old color to secure it in place and make sure there are no large loose loops hanging free inside your work. You will also need to ensure the yarn crocheted over does not show through your stitch holes. Then, once it is time to use the old color again, it is close by, ready to be used. *(images 1 & 2)*

For color changes occurring over longer distances, I recommend using a cut and tie technique. After using the invisible color change technique, cut the old color leaving a yarn tail. Tie the yarn tails of the old color and the new color together to secure them. *(image 3)*

Clean Stripe Technique

This technique may be used to give a crisp straight edge to your color changes. The technique is used as part of the Swan pattern. After performing your invisible color change you will then make a round of slip stitches through the front loops of the previous round. Keep the tension of your slip stitches loose. The stitches of the next round will then be made through the back loops of your slip stitches **and also** the back loops of the round before your slip stitches. *(images 1 - 6)*

Hints and Tips for Working with Chenille Yarn

When I first started using chenille, I had to learn a few of its quirks and differences compared to cotton or wool. Within this section I will cover a few of the basics to ensure you don't get frustrated, or too covered in fluff.

How to Prevent Shedding

There is more than one way to reduce the amount of shedding from your chenille. My preferred technique is to tie knots in the yarn tails at the start and end of the work. In order to do this, I leave a slightly longer tail when starting a piece. Make a knot approximately 2 inches (5 cm) away from the end of the yarn tail and then another a further 2 inches (5 cm) above this.

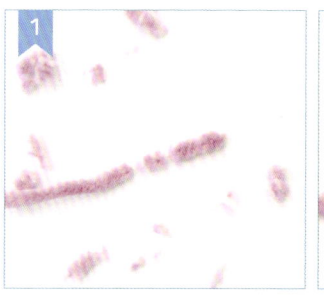
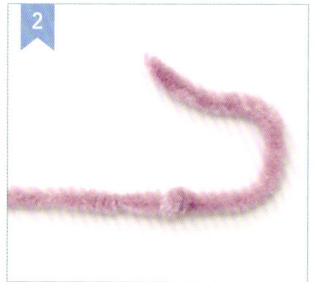

Another method involves passing a flame over the end of the inner core of the chenille. This technique scares me slightly, so I prefer the technique described above instead.

Magic Ring Alternative

Using a magic ring can be more difficult with chenille yarn. Sometimes the yarn refuses to slide through the stitches and if you pull too hard it can snap. An alternative to the magic ring would be to chain 2 and then make the indicated number of stitches (for example 8 single crochet) into the 2nd chain from your hook. You can then continue to work in the round as normal. *(images 1 - 3)*

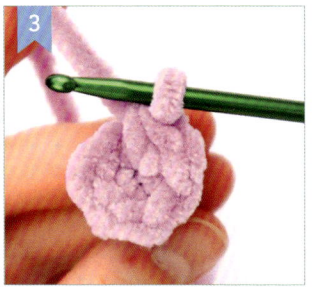

Magic Ring Assist

You can help your magic ring to close by adding a scrap piece of cotton to the base of your ring as it is formed. After sliding the stitches down to tighten the ring, the cotton can be removed or crocheted over. *(images 1 - 5)*

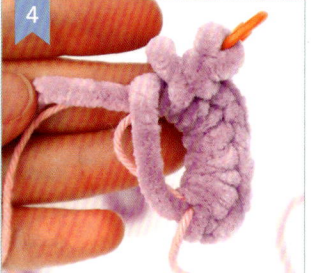

How to Secure Yarn Tails

Chenille is a soft and slippery fiber, so to secure yarn tails I tend to do two things. Firstly, I like to crochet over yarn tails as pieces are joined together. This means not having to weave in yarn tails; however, unlike cotton, crocheting over the yarn tails or weaving them in may not always be enough to secure the chenille, so secondly, I like to knot any loose ends together inside my work. This helps to prevent unravelling and also protects against shedding.

How to Sew Pieces Together

However tempting it may seem, **DO NOT** sew using the chenille. If you sew using the chenille yarn tail you will find that it snags, sheds and snaps frequently. Instead, if you need to sew any pieces together, I recommend using either a fine cotton (such as Hobbii 8/4 cotton) or my personal favorite, dental floss. PTFE dental floss is strong, very fine and becomes almost invisible when used to sew chenille together. The minty scent is an added bonus.

NO-SEW TECHNIQUES

How to Close a Piece with Single Crochet

For many of the limbs in this book, you will be asked to close off your work using a row of single crochet stitches. This technique gives you a flat row of single crochet stitches at the end of your work which is then used to perform a simple no-sew attachment later. It is possible to perform a no-sew join without closing a limb first; however, you will find the limb will not lie against the body fully using this method. By closing the limbs prior to joining them, you get an arm or leg that will sit nicely against the body.

Orientation is important prior to closing so that the limbs will align correctly with the body. Most patterns will prompt you to move your position by making or removing stitches or describe how the closing single crochet stitches should sit in relation to, for example, the decrease rows of a foot or arm.

To close limbs with an even number of stitches in the last round, start by making a ch 1, then fold the end of your work flat so that half the stitches sit on top of the other half, lining up the stitches. Next, insert your hook through the next stitch and then also through the corresponding stitch behind it, yarn over and pull a loop through both layers, then yarn over and pull through all loops on your hook, completing a single crochet. Repeat this across the entire top of the limb to close. For example, if you were closing a limb with 8 stitches in the final round, you would ch 1 (which will not count as a stitch), make 4 single crochet stitches across both layers, and then fasten off. I recommend crocheting over the yarn tails when the limb is eventually attached to the body, rather than weaving them in. *(images 1 - 4)*

To close a limb with an odd number of stitches in the last round, you do **not** ch 1 at the start of the closure; instead, you exclude one of the stitches (it is not worked into). Start by folding your work flat so that you have an even number of stitches sitting on top of each other (lined up) with the last stitch of the final round excluded, then you single crochet across the entire top of the limb, through the lined up stitches only. For example, if you were closing a limb with 9 stitches in the final round, you would fold the work flat, make 4 single crochet stitches across both layers (leaving that one stitch unworked) and then fasten off. *(images 5 & 6)*

Simple No-Sew Attachment

This is by far the most common method of no-sew attachment and one you are likely familiar with already. Essentially, this technique involves making single crochet stitches across multiple layers to join two pieces together. Most of the animals' arms in this book are joined using this method, so we will use attaching an arm as an example to explain the technique. To attach an arm to the body, you place the 4 closing stitches of the limb in front of the next 4 stitches of the body, aligning them. Orientation is important prior to joining, so the pattern will explain how to align the piece before attaching it to the body (for example, decreases point toward the body). Insert your hook through the next stitch on the arm and then the next stitch on the body, yarn over and pull a loop though both layers, then yarn over and pull through all loops on your hook, completing a single crochet stitch. This is repeated 3 more times to complete the attachment. *(images 1 & 2)*

Connecting Pieces with a Chain and How to Prevent Gaps

Connecting pieces with a chain is another common method for attaching two pieces together. For example, you use this technique to join the ears of the Calico Cat and Fox. You are instructed to make the first ear and then fasten off. The second ear is then made, but instead of fastening off, you make a chain and then crochet into the first ear. The chain acts like a bridge between both pieces. You then work around the rest of the first ear, back across the chain, around the second ear, and then back across the other side of the chain. This gives you an hourglass shaped piece.

It is common for gaps to form where the chain meets each piece. If you have mastered the above technique, you may want to give the following technique a try to prevent gaps. After you have made your joining chain, work around the first ear as previously described. To prevent a gap when going to work across the chain, insert your hook back through the same stitch you made the last stitch into on the first ear, then through the first chain stitch, and make a single crochet across both layers. Because you are working into a stitch you have previously worked into, making this stitch will not alter your overall stitch count, and creates a nice tight join across the gap. Work across the remaining chains. To prevent the next gap, insert your hook back through the final chain you have just worked into, then through the next stitch on the second ear, and make a single crochet across both layers. Repeat this technique when you work across the other side of the chain. This technique can be a little fiddly when starting out, so it is important to make sure you still have the correct stitch count when you finish the round.

Working Around an Opening and Corner Stitches

For many of the designs, such as the Bear and the Elephant, you create an opening in the head which will then become the attachment point for creating the body. A common example in the book is an opening that consists of 6 single crochet stitches and 6 chain stitches. Because the opening is made between two rounds, you also create two gaps in your work where the chain and single crochet stitches meet. Throughout the book I refer to these as "corner spaces". When starting to make the body, you will be asked to make stitches into these corner spaces as part of the first round. These corner stitches are marked with stitch markers in the step-by-step photos for clarity. If you do not work in the corner spaces, you will get holes in your work. *(images 1 - 3)*

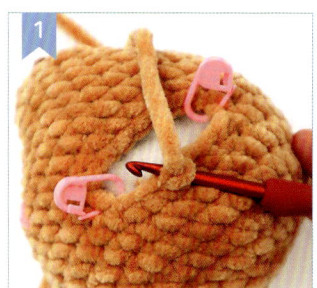

When working your first round around the corner spaces, it can be useful to remove some stuffing from this area for the first few rounds. This prevents stuffing from catching in your stitches.

Anchoring Techniques

Some pieces have more than one no-sew attachment point. The second attachment point is used to anchor the piece to another, often larger, piece and is therefore referred to as anchoring. I have developed this technique to help give additional shaping or prevent wobbly heads without having to sew stitches. For some of the smaller designs, front loops are left unworked to show where to perform the anchoring attachment, whilst in the bigger and more advanced designs you work back through the side of the head or body, into stitch holes that are not marked. Below, I will take you through examples of each of these types of anchors.

Basic Anchoring

Both the Duckling and the Baby Panda are examples of where we work back though unworked front loops to perform the anchoring. For the Baby Panda, you anchor the head to the body to prevent a wobbly head and make the face look slightly upwards.

In Round 9 of the Baby Panda's head you leave two front loops unworked and mark these with stitch markers to be worked into later. You then complete the head and go on to start making the body. In Round 3 of the body you then anchor the head to the body. This is done by folding the body back toward the head, inserting our hook through the first marked front loop on the head, then through the next stitch on the body and making a single crochet across both layers. You repeat this one more time in the second marked front loop on the head, then continue making the body. The head is now secure and should not wobble. Overall, this is a fairly simple but effective technique. *(images 1 - 4)*

More Complex Anchoring

A more advanced example of anchoring can be found in the Puppy and Bunny patterns when making the back legs. In Round 6 of the Puppy's back legs you will be asked to fold the leg back toward the body. You are then directed to insert your hook into the body and then out again through the two stitch holes closest to the next stitch on the leg. Finally, you insert your hook through the next stitch on the back leg and form a single crochet across all layers. The exact position to go through the body is not specified as this may vary slightly. It is more important that after performing the anchoring the leg sits flush against the body. *(images 1 - 5)*

Using this technique means the Puppy's legs do not flop downwards but instead are held in place. It also provides additional shaping to the leg.

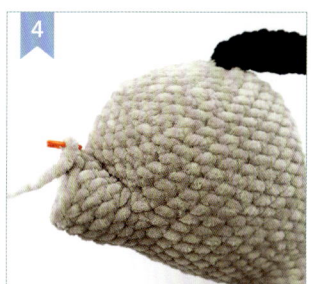

PROJECTS

ACACIA THE BEAR

Bee keeping is Acacia the Bear's passion. Her garden is full of lavender and wildflowers to keep her hives happy. Of course, the honey is a nice bonus.

Skill Level: Intermediate
Sewing Level: No-sew

Finished Size: 24 cm

Yarn:

Hobbii Honey Bunny (3.5 oz, 131 yds / 100 g, 120 m)
Hobbii Toucan (3.5 oz, 131 yds / 100 g, 120 m)
Main Color (MC): Honey Bunny in Nougat (09) for Arms, Legs, Head & Body – 1 ball
Color A: Toucan in Sky Blue (21) for Arms & Body – 1 ball
Color B: Toucan in Cotton Candy (16) for Cheeks – small amount
Color C: Toucan in Cappuccino (30) for Nose – small amount
Color D: Honey Bunny in Black (34) for bees in sweater – small amount
Color E: Honey Bunny in Lemon Curd (22) for bees in sweater – small amount
Color F: Honey Bunny in White (01) for bees in sweater – small amount

Materials:

G-6 (4.00 mm) hook
Two 8 mm oval safety eyes
Stuffing
Stitch markers
Yarn needle
Scissors
Black embroidery floss

Note: This design is made using the X stitch single crochet technique. Using the classic V stitch single crochet may slightly alter the position and look of the colorwork.

Orientation Check Points

Read these instructions carefully prior to starting the next round. You may be asked to alter the position of the start of the round before continuing.

Special Stitches:

Front Post Half Double Crochet (FPhdc):
Starting with a loop on your hook, yarn over and insert hook front to back through the gap on the right-hand side of the next stitch, then back to front through the gap on the left-hand side of the stitch (around the post of the stitch). Yarn over and pull a loop through (3 loops on hook). Yarn over and pull through all three loops on hook.

Back Post Half Double Crochet (BPhdc):
Starting with a loop on your hook, yarn over and insert hook back to front through the gap on the right-hand side of the next stitch, then front to back through the gap on the left-hand side of the stitch (around the post of the stitch). Yarn over and pull a loop through (3 loops on hook). Yarn over and pull through all three loops on hook.

Puff Stitch (puff):
Starting with a loop on your hook, yarn over and insert hook in the next stitch. Yarn over and pull a loop through (3 loops on hook). Yarn over and pull through 2 loops on hook (2 loops remain on hook). Repeat this process into the **same stitch** 4 more times (6 loops remain on hook). Yarn over and pull through all loops on hook.

ARM (Make 2)

Round 1: With MC, make a magic ring, 6 sc in ring. (6 sc)

Round 2: Inc in each st around. (12 sc)

Round 3: Sc in each st around. (12 sc)

Round 4: Sc in each of next 3 sts, puff in next st, sc in each of next 8 sts. (11 sc & 1 puff)

Round 5: [Dec] 3 times, sc in each of next 6 sts. (9 sc)

Change to Color A.

Round 6: Sc in each st around. (9 sc)

Round 7: Working in **back loops** only, sc in each st around. (9 sc)

Rounds 8-10: *(3 rounds)* Sc in each st around. (9 sc)

Sc in next st *(to move the end of round to side of Arm)*. Stuff lower 2/3 of Arm.

Closing Row: Flatten Arm; working through both layers *(to close opening)*, sc in each of next 4 sts. (4 sc)

Fasten off.

Sleeve Edging:

With hand facing upwards, attach Color A to an unworked front loop on Round 6 of Arm.

Round 1: Working in unworked **front loops** only, [sc in each of next 2 sts, inc in next st] 3 times. (12 sc)

Round 2: Sl st in each st around. (12 sl st)

Fasten off and weave in end. *(images 1 & 2)*

LEG (Make 2)

Round 1: With MC, make a magic ring, 8 sc in ring. (8 sc)

Round 2: Inc in each st around. (16 sc)

Round 3: Sc in each of next 6 sts, inc in each of next 4 sts, sc in each of next 6 sts. (20 sc)

Rounds 4-6: *(3 rounds)* Sc in each st around. (20 sc)

Stuff foot of Leg.

Round 7: Sc in each of next 4 sts, [dec] 6 times, sc in each of next 4 sts. (14 sc)

Round 8: Sc in each of next 3 sts, [dec] 4 times, sc in each of next 3 sts. (10 sc)

Rounds 9-12: *(4 rounds)* Sc in each st around. (10 sc)

Stuff lower half of Leg.

Closing Row: Flatten Leg, ch 1; working through both layers *(to close opening)*, sc in each of next 5 sts. (5 sc)

HEAD

Round 1: With MC, make a magic ring, 8 sc in ring. (8 sc)

Round 2: Inc in each st around. (16 sc)

Rounds 3-4: *(2 rounds)* Sc in each st around. (16 sc)

Round 5: Sc in each of next 4 sts, hdc-inc in each of next 8 sts, sc in each of next 4 sts. (8 sc & 16 hdc)

Round 6: Sc in each of next 4 sts, [sc in next st, inc in next st] 4 times, [inc in next st, sc in next st] 4 times, sc in each of next 4 sts. (32 sc)

Round 7: Sc in each of next 4 sts, [inc in next st, sc in each of next 2 sts] 4 times, [sc in each of next 2 sts, inc in next st] 4 times, sc in each of next 4 sts. (40 sc)

Rounds 8-10: *(3 rounds)* Sc in each st around. (40 sc)

Orientation Check Point

The next round should start centrally at the base of the Head. If needed, move the start of round forward (by making additional single crochet stitches), or back (by removing single crochet stitches) to allow for this.

Note: In the next round, you will make the Ears and start to make the opening for the Body. To mark the position of each Ear, place markers on the 13th, 15th, 26th, and 28th stitches of Round 10 (see photo; these stitches are the skipped stitches in the next round). The double crochet clusters in Round 11 will not be worked in again and are not included in overall stitch count.

Round 11: Sc in each of next 12 sts, skip next st, 8 dc in **front loop** of next st *(First Ear)*, skip next st; PM on unworked back loop behind First Ear; sc in each of next 10 sts, skip next st, 8 dc in **front loop** of next st *(Second Ear)*, skip next st; PM on unworked back loop behind Second Ear, sc in each of next 9 sts, ch 6, skip next 3 sts. *(images 3 - 6)*

Round 12: Skip next 3 sts *(Body opening)*, sc in next st; move start of round marker to 4th ch of ch-6 from Round 11; sc in each of next 8 sts; removing markers as you encounter them, sc in next skipped st from previous round, sc in **back loop** behind First Ear, sc in next skipped st from previous round; sc in each of next 10 sts; removing markers as you encounter them, sc in next skipped st from previous round, sc in **back loop** behind Second Ear, sc in next skipped st from previous round; sc in each of next 9 sts; working in ch-6, sc in each of next 3 ch. (37 sc & 3 ch-sts) *(images 7 - 9)*

As you work through the marked sts revome the markers. Do not fasten off.

Face Details

1. Insert safety eyes on Round 5 with a gap of 10 hdc between them.

2. With black embroidery floss, embroider small eyebrows 2 rounds above the safety eyes.

3. With Color B, embroider small cheeks on the lower outer aspect of the safety eyes.

4. With Color C, embroider the nose, starting through the magic ring and continuing over the 2 rounds above, forming a triangular shape. Make one long horizontal stitch across the top of the nose, then make a vertical stitch down from the bottom of the nose. *(images 10 - 13)*

Stuff Head and continue to stuff as you go. Continue with Head.

Round 13: Working in ch-6, sc in each of next 3 ch, sc in each remaining st around. (40 sc)

Round 14: Sc in each st around. (40 sc)

Round 15: [Sc in each of next 3 sts, dec] 8 times. (32 sc)

Round 16: [Sc in each of next 2 sts, dec] 8 times. (24 sc)

Round 17: [Sc in next st, dec] 8 times. (16 sc)

Round 18: [Dec] 8 times. (8 sc)

Fasten off, leaving a long tail for sewing. Use yarn needle to weave yarn tail through front loops of final round and pull to close.

BODY

Note: In the next round, you will be working around the Body opening made in Rounds 11 and 12 of the Head, starting in the ch-6. The stitch markers in the photos mark the corner spaces of the Body opening. (images 14 - 16)

Round 1: Attach MC at center back of Body opening *(3 ch-sts away from next corner space)*, sc in same ch, sc in each of next 2 ch, inc in next corner space between rounds, sc in each of next 6 sts, inc in next corner space between rounds, sc in each of next 3 ch. (16 sc)

Change to Color A.

Round 2: [Sc in next st, inc in next st] 8 times. (24 sc)

Orientation Check Point

The next round should start at the center back of the Body. If needed, move the start of round forward (by making additional single crochet stitches), or back (by removing single crochet stitches) to allow for this. If you need to remove stitches that include an increase, make sure you remake the increase so you continue to have the correct stitch count.

*Note: In the next round, you will attach the Arms. When attaching each Arm, hold the closing stitches of the Arm against the next stitches on the Body with the Arm puff stitch facing outwards. Work the "attaching" stitches through the Arm (in both loops) and the Body (in **back loop** only) together, across both layers.*

Round 3: Working in **back loops** only, sc in each of next 4 sts; *(Attach First Arm)* working on First Arm (in both loops) & Body (in **back loop** only), sc in each of next 4 sts; working on Body only (in **back loops** only), sc in each of next 8 sts; *(Attach Second Arm)* working on Second Arm (in both loops) & Body (in **back loop** only), sc in each of next 4 sts; working on Body only (in **back loops** only), sc in each of next 4 sts. (24 sc) *(images 17 & 18)*

Round 4: [Sc in each of next 2 sts, inc in next st] 8 times. (32 sc)

Round 5: Sc in each st around. (32 sc)

Round 6: Sc in each of next 17 sts; change to Color D, sc in next st; change to Color E, sc in each of next 2 sts; change to Color A, sc in each remaining st around. (32 sc)

Round 7: [Sc in each of next 3 sts, inc in next st] 8 times. (40 sc)

Round 8: Sc in each of next 14 sts; change to Color E, sc in each of next 2 sts; change to Color D, sc in next st, change to Color A, sc in each remaining st around. (40 sc)

Round 9: Sc in each st around. (40 sc)
Do not fasten off.

Bee Details

1. With Color D, embroider 2 vertical stripes on each bee.

2. With Color F, embroider a small V shape on the top of each bee to look like wings. *(image 19)*

Continue with Body.

Orientation Check Point

The next round should start at the center back of the Body. If needed, move the start of round forward (by making additional single crochet stitches), or back (by removing single crochet stitches) to allow for this.

Change to MC.

*Note: In the next round, you will attach the Legs. When attaching each Leg, hold the closing stitches of the Leg against the next stitches on the Body so that the foot points towards the front of the Bear once attached. Work each "attaching" stitch through the Leg (in both loops) and the Body (in **back loop** only) together, across both layers.*

Round 10: Working in **back loops** only, sc in each of next 8 sts; *(Attach First Leg)* working on First Leg (in both loops) & Body (in **back loop** only), sc in each of next 5 sts; working on Body only (in **back loops** only), sc in each of next 14 sts; *(Attach Second Leg)* working on Second Leg (in both loops) & Body (in **back loop** only), sc in each of next 5 sts; working on Body only (in **back loops** only), sc in each of next 8 sts. (40 sc) *(image 20)*

Round 11: Puff in next st, sc in each remaining st around. (1 puff & 39 sc) Stuff Body and continue to stuff as you go.

Round 12: [Sc in each of next 3 sts, dec] 8 times. (32 sc)

Orientation Check Point

The next round should start at the center back of the Body. If needed, move the start of round forward (by making additional single crochet stitches), or back (by removing single crochet stitches) to allow for this. If you need to remove stitches that include a decrease, make sure you remake the decrease so you continue to have the correct stitch count.

Note: In the next round, you will anchor the Legs to the Body, working through the side of each Leg. When anchoring each Leg, hold the side of the Leg against the next stitches on the Body. Work each "attaching" stitch through the two closest stitch holes on the Leg (inside then outside) and into the next stitch on the Body together, across both layers.

Round 13: [Sc in each of next 2 sts, dec] 2 times; *(Attach First Leg)* working on First Leg & Body, sc in each of next 2 sts; working on Body only, [dec, sc in each of next 2 sts] 3 times, dec; *(Attach Second Leg)* working on Second Leg & Body, sc in each of next 2 sts; working on Body only, dec, sc in each of next 2 sts, dec. (24 sc) *(images 21 & 22)*

Round 14: [Sc in next st, dec] 8 times. (16 sc)

Round 15: [Dec] 8 times. (8 sc)

Fasten off, leaving a long tail for sewing. Use yarn needle to weave yarn tail through front loops of final round and pull to close. *(image 23)*

Sweater Edging

With the Head pointing down and the back facing you, attach Color A to an unworked front loop on Round 9 of Body. *(image 24)*

Round 1: Working in unworked **front loops** only, [sc in each of next 4 sts, inc in next st] 8 times. (48 sc)

Round 2: Sl st in each st around. (48 sl st)

Fasten off and weave in end.

COLLAR

Note: Keep your tension quite loose while making the collar to prevent it from curling upwards.

With the Head pointing down and the back facing you, attach Color A to an unworked front loop on Round 2 of Body. *(image 25)*

Round 1: Ch 2 *(does not count as a st)*; working in unworked front loops only, [hdc in each of next 2 sts, hdc-inc in next st] 8 times. (32 hdc)

Round 2: [FPhdc, BPhdc] 16 times. (32 sts) *(images 26 & 27)*

Round 3: Sl st in each st around. (32 sl st)
Fasten off and weave in end.

MEI THE BUNNY

Mei's favourite time of year is the spring. Watching the cherry blossoms float on the wind fills her with joy. She loves to leap as the petals dance around her.

Skill Level: Intermediate
Sewing Level: No-sew

Finished Size: 28 cm

Yarn:

Hobbii Honey Bunny (3.5 oz, 131 yds / 100 g, 120 m)

Main Color (MC): White (01) for Ears, Tail, Head, Front Legs, Body & Back Legs – 2 balls

Color A: Hint of Pink (50) for Ears, Nose & Flower – 1 ball

Hobbii Toucan (3.5 oz, 131 yds / 100 g, 120 m)

Color B: Cotton Candy (16) for Cheeks – small amount (optional)

Materials:

G-6 (4.00 mm) hook
Two 8 mm oval safety eyes
Stuffing
Stitch markers
Yarn needle
Scissors
Black embroidery floss
Ribbon – 10" (25 cm) long, ¾" (2 cm) wide

Orientation Check Points

Read these instructions carefully prior to starting the next round. You may be asked to alter the position of the start of the round before continuing.

Special Stitches:

Picot Stitch (PICOT):

Starting with a loop on your hook, chain 3, then slip stitch into the 3rd chain from hook.

INNER EAR (Make 2)

Round 1: With Color A, ch 17; sc in 2nd ch from hook, sc in each of next 5 ch, hdc in each of next 5 ch, dc in each of next 4 ch, 6 dc in last ch; working on other side of starting ch, dc in each of next 4 ch, hdc in each of next 5 ch, sc in each of next 5 ch, inc in last ch. (13 sc, 10 hdc & 14 dc) Change to MC.

Round 2: Inc in next st, sc in each of next 5 sts, hdc in each of next 5 sts, dc in each of next 4 sts, dc-inc in each of next 6 sts, dc in each of next 4 sts, hdc in each of next 5 sts, sc in each of next 5 sts, inc in each of next 2 sts. (16 sc, 10 hdc & 20 dc) Fasten off and weave in end.

OUTER EAR (Make 2)

Round 1: With MC, ch 17; sc in 2nd ch from hook, sc in each of next 5 ch, hdc in each of next 5 ch, dc in each of next 4 ch, 6 dc in last ch; working on other side of starting ch, dc in each of next 4 ch, hdc in each of next 5 ch, sc in each of next 5 ch, inc in last ch. (13 sc, 10 hdc & 14 dc)

Round 2: Inc in next st, sc in each of next 5 sts, hdc in each of next 5 sts, dc in each of next 4 sts, dc-inc in each of next 6 sts, dc in each of next 4 sts, hdc in each of next 5 sts, sc in each of next 5 sts, inc in each of next 2 sts. (16 sc, 10 hdc & 20 dc) Do not fasten off.

Continue to Round 3 to join Inner and Outer Ears together. *(image 1)*

Round 3: *(Joining Inner Ear & Outer Ear)* With right sides facing out, place Outer Ear on top of Inner Ear; working on Inner Ear & Outer Ear together, sc in each st around across both layers. (46 sc) *(image 2)*

Fasten off and weave in end. Alternatively, crochet over end when Ears are attached to Head.

TAIL

Round 1: With MC, make a magic ring, 8 sc in ring. (8 sc)

Round 2: Inc in each st around. (16 sc)

Rounds 3-5: *(3 rounds)* Sc in each st around. (16 sc)

Stuff Tail.

Round 6: [Dec] 8 times. (8 sc)

Fasten off and weave in end. Alternatively, crochet over end when Tail attached to Body.

HEAD

Round 1: With MC, make a magic ring, 6 sc in ring. (6 sc)

Round 2: [3 sc in next st, sc in next st] 3 times. (12 sc)

Round 3: Sc in each st around. (12 sc)

Round 4: Sc in next st, 3 sc in next st, [sc in each of next 3 sts, 3 sc in next st] 2 times, sc in each of next 2 sts. (18 sc)

Round 5: Sc in each st around. (18 sc)

Round 6: Sc in each of next 2 sts, 3 sc in next st, [sc in each of next 5 sts, 3 sc in next st] 2 times, sc in each of next 3 sts. (24 sc)

Round 7: Sc in each of next 11 sts, hdc-inc in each of next 8 sts, sc in each of next 5 sts. (16 sc & 16 hdc)

PM on 2 middle hdc-sts *(marks center of Head and will help with orientation)*.

Round 8: Sc in each of next 11 sts, [sc in next st, inc in next st] 8 times, sc in each of next 5 sts. (40 sc)

Rounds 9-11: *(3 rounds)* Sc in each st around. (40 sc)

> **Orientation Check Point**
> The next round should start centrally at the base of the Head (directly opposite the marked central increase sts in Round 7). If needed, move the start of round forward (by making additional single crochet stitches), or back (by removing single crochet stitches) to allow for this.

Note: In the next round, you will attach the Ears at the top of the Head with 4 stitches in between. It may be helpful to mark out the position of the Ears with stitch markers (as in photo). When attaching each Ear, hold the base of the Ear against the next stitches on the Head with the Inner Ear facing outwards. Work the "attaching" stitches through the Ear and the Head together, across both layers. *(image 3)*

Round 12: Sc in each of next 15 sts; *(Attach First Ear)* working on First Ear & Head, sc in each of next 3 sts; working on Head only, sc in each of next 4 sts; *(Attach Second Ear)* working on Second Ear & Head, sc in each of next 3 sts; working on Body only, sc in each of next 15 sts. (40 sc) *(images 4 & 5)*

Rounds 13-14: *(2 rounds)* Sc in each st around. (40 sc)

Do not fasten off.

Face Details

1. Insert safety eyes on either side of half double crochet stitches of Round 7.

2. With black thread, embroider eyelashes around safety eyes (optional).

3. With Color A, embroider a small nose through the magic ring of the Head and over Round 1, forming a triangular shape. Finish with one long horizontal stitch across the top of the nose.

4. With Color B, embroider cheeks on the lower outer aspect of the eyes (straight stitches over 1 round). *(image 6)*

Stuff Head and continue to stuff as you go.

Continue with Head.

Round 15: [Sc in each of next 3 sts, dec] 8 times. (32 sc)

Round 16: [Sc in each of next 2 sts, dec] 8 times. (24 sc)

> **Orientation Check Point**
> In the next round, you will create the opening for the Body. The round should start centrally at the base of the Head. If needed, move the start of round forward (by making additional single crochet stitches), or back (by removing single crochet stitches) to allow for this. If you need to remove stitches that include a decrease, make sure you remake the decrease so you continue to have the correct stitch count.

Round 17: Sc in each of next 3 sts, [sc in next st, dec] 6 times, ch 4, skip next 6 sts *(Body opening; **this will extend beyond end of round**)*. *(image 7)*

Note: The next stitch you make will be the new start of round.

Round 18: [Dec] 6 times; working in ch-4, [dec] 2 times. (8 sc)

Fasten off, leaving a long tail for sewing. Use yarn needle to weave yarn tail through front loops of final round and pull to close. *(image 8)*

FRONT LEGS

First Front Leg

Round 1: With MC, make a magic ring, 6 sc in ring. (6 sc)

Round 2: Inc in each st around. (12 sc)

Round 3: [Sc in next st, inc in next st] 6 times. (18 sc)

Rounds 4-6: *(3 rounds)* Sc in each st around. (18 sc)

Round 7: Sc in each of next 5 sts, [dec] 4 times, sc in each of next 5 sts. (14 sc)

Stuff First Front Leg and continue to stuff as you go.

Rounds 8-13: *(6 rounds)* Sc in each st around. (14 sc)

Fasten off. *(image 9)*

Second Front Leg

Rounds 1-13: *(13 rounds)* Repeat Rounds 1-13 of First Front Leg; work additional sc to move the end of round to side of Second Front Leg.

Do not fasten off. Continue to join the Front Legs with a chain.

Round 14: *(Joining Front Legs)* From Second Front Leg, ch 4; working on First Front Leg, sc in st on inner side of Leg *(so feet face same direction)*, sc in each of next 13 sts; working in ch-4, sc in each of next 4 ch; working on Second Front Leg, sc in each of next 14 sts. (32 sc & 4 ch-sts)

Round 15: Working in ch-4, sc in each of next 4 ch, sc in each of next 3 sts, [dec] 4 times, sc in each of next 10 sts, [dec] 4 times, sc in each of next 3 sts. (28 sc) *(images 10-12)*

Note: In the next round, you will attach the Head. The technique is the same as for the Puppy. Contrasting colors are used in the photos for clarity. When attaching the Head, hold the 6 skipped single crochet stitches on the base of the Head against the next stitches on the front of the Front Legs. Work the "attaching" stitches through the Head (from inside to outside) and the Front Legs together, across both layers.

Round 16: Sc in each of next 6 sts, dec, sc in each of next 2 sts, dec, sc in next st; *(Attach Head)* working on Head *(in skipped sc stitches)* & Front Legs, sc in each of next 6 sts; working on Front Legs only, sc in next st, dec, sc in each of next 2 sts, dec, sc in each of next 2 sts. (24 sc) *(images 13 & 14)*

Note: In the next round, you will crochet into the remaining unworked stitches of the Head. The attaching stitches from the previous round and the slip stitches made in the next round (to prevent gaps) will not be worked into again and are not included in overall stitch count.

Round 17: Sc in each of next 11 sts, sl st across same 2 sts as first attaching st; working on Head, inc in next corner space *(marked by a stitch marker in photo)*; working in ch-4 on Head, sc in each of next 4 ch; inc in next corner space on Head *(marked by a stitch marker in photo)*; sl st across same 2 sts as last attaching st; working on Front Legs, sc in each of next 7 sts. (26 sc) *(images 15 & 16)*

Do not fasten off. Continue with Body.

BODY

Round 18: [Sc in each of next 6 sts, inc in next st, sc in each of next 5 sts, inc in next st] 2 times. (30 sc)

Round 19: [Sc in each of next 4 sts, inc in next st] 6 times. (36 sc)

Rounds 20-21: *(2 rounds)* Sc in each st around. (36 sc)

Round 22: [Sc in each of next 5 sts, inc in next st] 6 times. (42 sc)

Rounds 23-24: *(2 rounds)* Sc in each st around. (42 sc)

Round 25: [Sc in each of next 6 sts, inc in next st] 6 times. (48 sc)

Rounds 26-27: *(2 rounds)* Sc in each st around. (48 sc) *(image 17)*

Orientation Check Point

In the next round, you will be making the openings for the Back legs. The round should start centrally at the base of the Body. If needed, move the start of round forward (by making additional single crochet stitches), or back (by removing single crochet stitches) to allow for this.

Round 28: Sc in each of next 2 sts, ch 7, skip next 7 sts *(First Back Leg opening)*, sc in each of next 30 sts, ch 7, skip next 7 sts *(Second Back Leg opening)*, sc in each of next 2 sts. (34 sc & 14 ch-sts) *(image 18)*

Round 29: Sc in each of next 2 sts; working in ch-7, sc in each of next 7 ch; sc in each of next 30 sts; working in ch-7, sc in each of next 7 ch; sc in each of next 2 sts. (48 sc)

Round 30: [Sc in each of next 6 sts, dec] 6 times. (42 sc)

Stuff Body and continue to stuff as you go.

Round 31: [Sc in each of next 5 sts, dec] 6 times. (36 sc)

Orientation Check Point

The next round should start centrally at the base of the Body. If needed, move the start of round forward (by making additional single crochet stitches), or back (by removing single crochet stitches) to allow for this. If you need to remove stitches that include a decrease, make sure you remake the decrease so you continue to have the correct stitch count.

Note: In the next round, you will attach the Tail. When attaching the Tail, flatten the last round of the Tail and hold it against the next stitches on the Body. Work the "attaching" stitches through both layers of the Tail and the Body together, across all three layers.

Round 32: Sc in each of next 2 sts, dec, [sc in each of next 4 sts, dec] 2 times; *(Attach Tail)* working on Tail & Body, sc in each of next 4 sts; working on Body only, dec, [sc in each of next 4 sts, dec] 2 times, sc in each of next 2 sts. (30 sc) *(image 19)*

Round 33: [Sc in each of next 3 sts, dec] 6 times. (24 sc)

Round 34: [Sc in each of next 2 sts, dec] 6 times. (18 sc)

Round 35: [Sc in next st, dec] 6 times. (12 sc)

Round 36: [Dec] 6 times. (6 sc)

Fasten off, leaving a long tail for sewing. Use yarn needle to weave yarn tail through front loops of final round and pull to close.

BACK LEG (Make 2 – one in each opening)

Note: In the next round, you will be working around a Leg opening made in Round 28 of the Body, starting in the skipped stitches. The stitch markers in the photo mark the corner spaces of the Back Leg opening. (image 20)

Round 1: With Front Legs & Head pointing down, attach MC to skipped st from Round 28 of Body on lower right side of Back Leg opening, sc in same st, sc in each of next 6 sts, dec across next corner space *(marked with stitch marker in photo)* and next ch, sc in each of next 5 ch, dec across next ch and next corner *space (marked* with stitch marker in photo). (14 sc) *(image 20)*

Rounds 2-5: *(4 rounds)* Sc in each st around. (14 sc)

Note: In the next round, you will anchor the Back Leg to the Body. When anchoring the Back Leg, fold the Leg up towards the backend of the Body so that the next stitches on the Leg are against the Body. Work each "attaching" stitch through the two closest stitch holes on the Body (inside then outside) and into the next stitch on the Back Leg together, across both layers.

Round 6: Sc in each of next 9 sts; fold Back Leg towards backend of Body; *(Attach Back Leg)* working on Body & Back Leg, sc in each of next 4 sts; working on Back Leg only, sc in next st. (14 sc) *(images 21 - 23)*

Round 7: [Dec] 4 times, sc in next st, inc in each of next 4 sts, sc in next st. (14 sc)

Round 8: Sc in next st, inc in each of next 2 sts, sc in each of next 4 sts, [dec] 2 times, sc in each of next 3 sts. (14 sc)

Stuff Back Leg and continue to stuff as you go.

Round 9: Sc in next st, inc in next st, sc in each of next 2 sts, inc in next st, sc in each of next 2 sts, dec, sc in each of next 2 sts, dec, sc in next st. (14 sc)

Round 10: Sc in each of next 3 sts, inc in each of next 2 sts, sc in each of next 4 sts, [dec] 2 times, sc in next st. (14 sc)

Round 11: Sc in each of next 2 sts, inc in each of next 4 sts, sc in each of next 8 sts. (18 sc)

Rounds 12-13: *(2 rounds)* Sc in each st around. (18 sc)

Round 14: Dec, sc in each of next 10 sts, [dec] 3 times. (14 sc)

Round 15: [Dec] 7 times. (7 sc)

Fasten off, leaving a long tail for sewing. Use yarn needle to weave yarn tail through front loops of final round and pull to close. *(image 24)*

FLOWER

Round 1: With Color A, make a magic ring, 5 sc in ring. (5 sc)

Round 2: (Sl st, ch 2, dc, PICOT, dc, ch 2, sl st) in each of next 5 sts.

Fasten off and weave in ends.

Thread the ribbon onto your yarn needle and pass it through the back of the Flower.

1. Tie the ribbon around the Bunny's Head like a headband.

2. Trim ends of ribbon.

DEBAKEY THE CAT

DeBakey the cat loves to catch mice. He can sit still for hours patiently waiting to pounce. His new collar has unfortunately been interfering with this hobby. Perhaps he will just have to chase some yarn instead.

Skill Level: Intermediate
Sewing Level: Low-sew

Finished Size: 26 cm

Yarn:

Hobbii Honey Bunny (3.5 oz, 131 yds / 100 g, 120 m)

Main Color (MC): White (01) for Head, Back Legs, Tail, Front Legs & Body - 2 balls

Color A: Silver (118) for First Ear, Tail & Second Front Leg - 1 ball

Color B: Nougat (09) for Second Ear & First Front Leg - 1 ball

Color C: Hint of Pink (50) for Front Legs & Back Legs - 1 ball

Color D: Turquoise (94) for Collar - small amount

Color E: Pastel Yellow (21) for Bell - small amount

Materials:

G-6 (4.00 mm) hook

Two 30 mm kawaii sinker safety eyes (alternatively, use 20 mm safety eyes with a 30 mm diameter circle of colored felt behind)

Stuffing

Stitch markers

Yarn needle

Scissors

White fingering weight cotton yarn – small amount (ex. Hobbii Friends 8/4 Cotton)

Pink fingering weight cotton yarn – small amount (ex. Hobbii Friends 8/4 Cotton)

Black embroidery floss

Foam roller (optional)

Orientation Check Points

Read these instructions carefully prior to starting the next round. You may be asked to alter the position of the start of the round before continuing.

EARS

First Ear

Round 1: With Color A, make a magic ring, 4 sc in ring. (4 sc)

Round 2: [Inc in next st, sc in next st] 2 times. (6 sc)

Round 3: [Inc in next st, sc in each of next 2 sts] 2 times. (8 sc)

Round 4: [Inc in next st, sc in each of next 3 sts] 2 times. (10 sc)

Round 5: [Inc in next st, sc in each of next 4 sts] 2 times. (12 sc)

Fasten off.

Second Ear

Rounds 1-5: *(5 rounds)* With Color B, repeat Rounds 1-5 of First Ear.

Do not fasten off. Continue with Head to join the Ears with a chain.

HEAD

Change to MC.

Round 6: *(Joining Ears)* Continuing on Second Ear, sl st in next st, ch 4; working on First Ear, sc in an inc st on Round 5; move start of round to st just made; change to Color A, sc in each of next 10 sts on First Ear; change to MC, sc in last st on First Ear; working in ch-4, sc in next ch, inc in each of next 2 ch, sc in last ch; working on Second Ear, sc in next st; change to Color B, sc in each of next 10 sts on Second Ear; change to MC, sc in next sl st on Second Ear; working on other side of ch-4, sc in next ch, inc in each of next 2 ch, sc in last ch. (36 sc) *(images 1 - 4)*

Round 7: Sc in each of next 2 sts; change to Color A, sc in each of next 3 sts, inc in each of next 2 sts, sc in each of next 3 sts; change to MC, sc in each of next 10 sts; change to Color B, sc in each of next 3 sts, inc in each of next 2 sts, sc in each of next 3 sts; change to MC, sc in each of next 8 sts. (40 sc)

Round 8: Sc in each of next 3 sts, change to Color A, sc in each of next 8 sts; change to MC, sc in each of next 3 sts, inc in next st, sc in each of next 4 sts, inc in next st, sc in each of next 3 sts; change to Color B, sc in each of next 8 sts; change to MC, sc in each of next 3 sts, inc in next st, sc in each of next 4 sts, inc in next st. (44 sc)

Round 9: Sc in each of next 4 sts; change to Color A, sc in each of next 2 sts, inc in each of next 2 sts, sc in each of next 2 sts; change to MC, sc in each of next 16 sts; change to Color B, sc in each of next 2 sts, inc in each of next 2 sts, sc in each of next 2 sts; change to MC, sc in each of next 12 sts. (48 sc)

Cut Color B and Color A and secure ends.

Rounds 10-11: *(2 rounds)* Sc in each st around. (48 sc)

Orientation Check Point
The next round should start centrally at the back of the Head. If needed, move the start of round forward (by making additional single crochet stitches), or back (by removing single crochet stitches) to allow for this.

Round 12: Sc in each of next 4 sts, [sc in each of next 3 sts, inc in next st] 4 times, sc in each of next 8 sts, [inc in next st, sc in each of next 3 sts] 4 times, sc in each of next 4 sts. (56 sc)

Rounds 13-14: *(2 rounds)* Sc in each st around. (56 sc)

Round 15: Sc in each of next 4 sts, [sc in each of next 4 sts, inc in next st] 4 times, sc in each of next 8 sts, [inc in next st, sc in each of next 4 sts] 4 times, sc in each of next 4 sts. (64 sc)

Rounds 16-20: *(5 rounds)* Sc in each st around. (64 sc)

Orientation Check Point
The next round should start centrally at the back of the Head. If needed, move the start of round forward (by making additional single crochet stitches), or back (by removing single crochet stitches) to allow for this.

Round 21: Sc in each of next 4 sts, [sc in each of next 4 sts, dec] 4 times, sc in each of next 8 sts, [dec, sc in each of next 4 sts] 4 times, sc in each of next 4 sts. (56 sc)

Insert safety eyes between Rounds 15 & 16, approximately 14 sts apart and in line with the ears. *(image 5)*

Start to stuff Head and continue to stuff as you go. Ears are not stuffed.

Round 22: Sc in each of next 4 sts, [sc in each of next 3 sts, dec] 4 times, sc in each of next 8 sts, [dec, sc in each of next 3 sts] 4 times, sc in each of next 4 sts. (48 sc)

Round 23: Sc in each of next 4 sts, [sc in each of next 2 sts, dec] 4 times, sc in each of next 8 sts, [dec, sc in each of next 2 sts] 4 times, sc in each of next 4 sts. (40 sc)

Round 24: Sc in each of next 4 sts, [sc in next st, dec] 4 times, sc in each of next 8 sts, [dec, sc in next st] 4 times, sc in each of next 4 sts. (32 sc)

Round 25: Sc in each of next 4 sts, [dec] 4 times, sc in each of next 8 sts, [dec] 4 times, sc in each of next 4 sts. (24 sc)

Round 26: Sc in each of next 2 sts, [dec, sc in next st] 2 times, dec, sc in each of next 4 sts, [dec, sc in next st] 2 times, dec, sc in each of next 2 sts. (18 sc)

Fasten off.

Nose

With pink fingering weight cotton yarn, embroider nose. Make straight horizontal stitches centrally between the safety eyes. To create a lazy bullion stitch, pass the yarn around your straight stitches multiple times, creating small loops. Snug the loops down and repeat until the entire length of the nose is covered (see Special Stitches section). Secure yarn ends. *(images 6 - 11)*

BACK LEG (Make 2)

Round 1: With Color C, make a magic ring, 8 sc in ring. (8 sc)

Round 2: Inc in each st around. (16 sc)

Change to MC.

Round 3: Sc in each of next 4 sts, inc in each of next 8 sts, sc in each of next 4 sts. (24 sc)

Rounds 4-5: *(2 rounds)* Sc in each st around. (24 sc)

Round 6: Sc in each of next 4 sts, [sc in each of next 2 sts, dec] 4 times, sc in each of next 4 sts. (20 sc)

Round 7: Sc in each of next 4 sts, [sc in next st, dec] 4 times, sc in each of next 4 sts. (16 sc)

Round 8: Sc in each of next 2 sts, [dec, sc in next st] 4 times, sc in each of next 2 sts. (12 sc)

Stuff foot of Back Leg.

Round 9: Sc in each of next 2 sts, [dec] 4 times, sc in each of next 2 sts. (8 sc)

> **Orientation Check Point**
> Flatten the top of the Back Leg so that the foot points upwards (perpendicular to the flattened end). You want the end of round to be to one side of the flattened end. If needed, work additional single crochet stitches to move the end of round to the side of the Leg.

Closing Row: Flatten Back Leg, ch 1; working through both layers *(to close opening)*, sc in each of next 4 sts. (4 sc)

Fasten off. *(image 12)*

TAIL

Round 1: With Color A, make a magic ring, 8 sc in ring. (8 sc)

Rounds 2-7: *(6 rounds)* Sc in each st around. (8 sc)

Change to MC. Stuff Tail and continue to stuff as you go.

Rounds 8-17: *(10 rounds)* Sc in each st around. (8 sc)

Round 18: Sc in each of next 4 sts; working in **back loops** only, sc in each of next 2 sts; PM on each unworked front loop; working in both loops, sc in each of next 2 sts. (8 sc)

Gradually reduce volume of stuffing used in last few rounds of Tail.

Rounds 19-23: *(5 rounds)* Sc in each st around. (8 sc)

> **Orientation Check Point**
> Flatten the top of the Tail so that the marked unworked front loops both face upwards, parallel to the flattened end. You want the end of round to be to one side of the flattened end. If needed, work additional single crochet stitches to move the end of round to the side of the Tail.

Closing Row: Flatten Tail, ch 1; working through both layers *(to close opening)*, sc in each of next 4 sts. (4 sc)

Fasten off. *(image 13)*

FRONT LEGS

First Front Leg

Round 1: With Color C, make a magic ring, 8 sc in ring. (8 sc)

Change to Color B.

Round 2: Inc in each st around. (16 sc)

Rounds 3-5: *(3 rounds)* Sc in each st around. (16 sc)

Round 6: Sc in each of next 4 sts, [dec] 4 times, sc in each of next 4 sts. (12 sc)

Rounds 7-9: *(3 rounds)* Sc in each st around. (12 sc)

Change to MC. Stuff Front Leg and continue to add stuffing as you go.

Rounds 10-15: *(8 rounds)* Sc in each st around. (12 sc)

Fasten off.

Second Front Leg

Round 1: With Color C, make a magic ring, 8 sc in ring. (8 sc)

Change to Color A.

Round 2: Inc in each st around. (16 sc)

Rounds 3-5: *(3 rounds)* Sc in each st around. (16 sc)

Round 6: Sc in each of next 4 sts, [dec] 4 times, sc in each of next 4 sts. (12 sc)

Round 7: Sc in each st around. (12 sc)

Change to MC. Stuff Front Leg and continue to add stuffing as you go.

Rounds 8-15: *(8 rounds)* Sc in each st around. (12 sc)

Fasten off. *(image 14)*

BODY

Round 1: With MC, make a magic ring, 8 sc in ring. (8 sc)

Round 2: Inc in each st around. (16 sc)

Round 3: Sc in each of next 4 sts, inc in each of next 4 sts, sc in each of next 4 sts, inc in each of next 4 sts. (24 sc)

Round 4: Sc in each of next 4 sts, [sc in next st, inc in next st] 4 times, sc in each of next 4 sts, [sc in next st, inc in next st] 4 times. (32 sc)

Round 5: Sc in each of next 4 sts, [sc in each of next 2 sts, inc in next st] 4 times, sc in each of next 4 sts, [sc in each of next 2 sts, inc in next st] 4 times. (40 sc)

Note: In the next round, you will attach the Tail and Back Legs. When attaching the Tail, hold the closing stitches of the Tail against the next stitches on the Body with the Tail stitch markers facing outwards. When attaching each Back Leg, hold the closing stitches of the Back Leg against the next stitches on the Body with the foot pointing outwards. Work the "attaching" stitches through the Tail or Back Leg and the Body together, across both layers.

Round 6: *(Attach Tail)* Working on Tail & Body, sc in each of next 4 sts; working on Body only, sc in each of next 10 sts; *(Attach First Back Leg)* working on First Back Leg & Body, sc in each of next 4 sts; working on Body only, sc in each of next 8 sts; *(Attach Second Back Leg)* working on Second Back Leg & Body, sc in each of next 4 sts; working on Body only, sc in each of next 10 sts. (40 sc) *(images 15 - 18)*

Rounds 7-11: *(5 rounds)* Sc in each st around. (40 sc)

Note: In the next round, you will anchor the Tail to the Body, through the marked unworked front loops of the Tail. When anchoring the Tail, hold the two marked front loops on Round 17 of the Tail against the next stitches on the Body. Work the "attaching" stitches through the Tail and the Body together, across both layers.

Round 12: Sc in each of next 2 sts; *(Attach Tail)* working on Tail *(in marked front loops)* & Body, sc in each of next 2 sts; working on Body only, sc in each of next 36 sts. (40 sc) *(images 19 - 21)*

> **Orientation Check Point**
> Make an additional single crochet stitch and move the start of round forward by one stitch.

Round 13: Sc in each of next 4 sts, [sc in each of next 2 sts, dec] 4 times, sc in each of next 4 sts, [dec, sc in each of next 2 sts] 4 times. (32 sc)

Rounds 14-15: *(2 rounds)* Sc in each st around. (32 sc)

Note: In the next round, you will attach the Front Legs. When attaching each Front Leg, hold the 4 sts at the back of the Leg (you will only work into these back 4 sts; the remaining sts are left unworked this round) against the next stitches on the Body with the foot pointing outwards. Work the "attaching" stitches through the Front Leg (from inside to outside) and the Body together, across both layers. *(image 22)*

Round 16: Sc in each of next 14 sts; *(Attach First Front Leg)* working on First Front Leg *(in back 4 sts)* & Body, sc in each of next 4 sts; working on Body only, sc in each of next 2 sts; *(Attach Second Front Leg)* working on Second Front Leg *(in back 4 sts)* & Body, sc in each of next 4 sts; working on Body only, sc in each of next 8 sts. (32 sc)

(images 23 - 25)

Stuff Body firmly and continue to stuff as you go.

Note: In the next round, you will crochet into the unworked stitches of each Front Leg. The attaching stitches of the Legs from the previous round (as shown with stitch markers in *image 24*) will not be worked into again and are not included in overall stitch count.

Round 17: Sc in each of next 6 sts, dec, sc in each of next 4 sts, dec; working on First Front Leg, sc in next st, dec, sc in each of next 2 sts, dec, sc in next st; working on Body, sc in each of next 2 sts: working on Second Front Leg, sc in next st, dec, sc in each of next 2 sts, dec, sc in next st; working on Body, dec, sc in each of next 4 sts, dec. (32 sc) *(images 26 - 28)*

Round 18: Sc in each st around. (32 sc)

Round 19: [Sc in each of next 2 sts, dec] 8 times. (24 sc)

Round 20: Sc in each st around. (24 sc)

Round 21: [Sc in each of next 2 sts, dec] 6 times. (18 sc)

Fasten off. *(image 29)*

COLLAR

Row 1: With Color D, ch 27, sc in 2nd ch from hook, sc in each of next 25 ch. (26 sc)

Row 2: Ch 1, turn, sc in each st across. (26 sc)

Fasten off.

BELL

Round 1: With Color E, make a magic ring, 6 sc in ring. (6 sc)

Round 2: Inc in each st around. (12 sc)

Rounds 3-5: *(3 rounds)* Sc in each st around. (12 sc)

Stuff Bell.

Round 6: [Inv-dec] 6 times. (6 sc)

Fasten off, leaving a long tail for sewing. Use yarn needle to weave yarn tail through front loops of final round and pull to close.

1. With black embroidery floss, embroider an I shape on Bell.

ASSEMBLY

1. Using white fingering weight cotton yarn, sew the Head to the Body. Ensure there is adequate stuffing around the neck prior to closing to prevent the Head from being floppy. Alternatively, foam rollers may be added to reinforce the neck. *(image 30)*

2. Sew Bell to Collar, slightly off center.

3. Place Collar around the neck and sew the ends together.

DAISY THE DUCKLING

Ducks should love water, but Daisy is not so sure. She would prefer to sit on the grass on a warm sunny day. Just in case of rain, she always wears a hat to keep her feathers dry.

Skill Level: Intermediate
Sewing Level: Low-sew

Finished Size: 16 cm

Yarn:

Hobbii Honey Bunny (3.5 oz, 131 yds/100 g, 120 m)

Main Color (MC): Pastel Yellow (21) for Tail, Head & Body - 1 ball

Color A: Gold Dust (27) for Feet & Beak - 1 ball

Color B: Candyfloss (45) for Petals of Hat - 1 ball

Color C: Shamrock (104) for Stem of Hat - small amount

Materials:

G-6 (4.00 mm) hook

Two 16 mm safety eyes

Stuffing

Stitch markers

Yarn needle

Scissors

Blush

Orientation Check Points

Read these instructions carefully prior to starting the next round. You may be asked to alter the position of the start of the round before continuing.

TAIL

Round 1: With MC, make a magic ring, 6 sc in ring. (6 sc)

Round 2: [Inc in next st, sc in each of next 2 sts] 2 times. (8 sc)

Fasten off and weave in end.

FOOT (Make 2)

Round 1: With Color A, ch 5; sc in 2nd ch from hook, sc in each of next 2 ch, 3 sc in last ch; working on other side of starting ch, sc in each of next 2 ch, inc in last ch. (10 sc)

Round 2: Sc in next st; working in **back loops** only, sc in each of next 2 sts; PM on each unworked front loop; working in both loops, sc in each of next 7 sts. (10 sc)

Round 3: Sc in each st around. (10 sc)

Round 4: [Sc in each of next 3 sts, dec] 2 times. (8 sc)

Round 5: Sc in each st around. (8 sc)

Round 6: [Sc in each of next 2 sts, dec] 2 times. (6 sc)

Do not stuff Foot.

Closing Row 1: Flatten Foot, ch 1; working through both layers *(to close opening)*, sc in each of next 3 sts. (3 sc)

Row 2: Ch 1, turn; working in **back loops** only, sc in each st across. (3 sc) Fasten off. *(image 1)*

HEAD

Round 1: With MC, make a magic ring, 8 sc in ring. (8 sc)

Round 2: Inc in each st around. (16 sc)

45

Round 3: [Sc in next st, inc in next st] 8 times. (24 sc)

Rounds 4-7: *(4 rounds)* Sc in each st around. (24 sc)

Round 8: Sc in each of next 10 sts; change to Color A, sc in each of next 4 sts; change to MC, sc in each of next 10 sts. (24 sc)

Note: In the next round, you will make the opening for the Beak.

Round 9: Sc in each of next 9 sts; change to Color A, sc in next st, ch 4, skip next 4 sts *(Beak opening)*, sc in next st; change to MC, sc in each of next 9 sts. (20 sc & 4 ch-sts)

Round 10: Sc in each of next 10 sts; working in ch-4, sc in each of next 4 ch; sc in each of next 10 sts. (24 sc)

Rounds 11-14: *(4 rounds)* Sc in each st around. (24 sc)

Do not fasten off. Remove hook and place marker in working loop to secure it. Continue to Beak.

BEAK

Note: In the next round, you will be working around the Beak opening made in Round 9 of the Head, starting in the skipped stitches of Round 8.

Round 1: Attach Color A in first Color A st of Round 8 of Head; sc in same st, sc in each of next 3 sts, inc in next corner space between rounds; working in ch-4, sc in each of next 4 ch; inc in next corner space between rounds. (12 sc)

Round 2: Sc in each st around. (12 sc)

Round 3: Sc in each of next 4 sts, dec] 2 times. (10 sc)

Fasten off, leaving a long tail for sewing Beak closed. *(images 2 - 4)*

1. To sew Beak closed, flatten the open end with the decreases at the corners and the two sets of 4 single crochet stitches lined up on top of each other. Sew through both layers of the single crochet stitches with a whip stitch to close. Do not sew in the corner decrease stitches. *(images 5 & 6)*

2. Insert safety eyes between Rounds 8 & 9 of the Head, one stitch away from the Beak. *(image 7)*

3. Insert hook in marked working loop of Head and continue with Body.

BODY

Note: In the next round, you will join the Tail at the end of the chain to create the Body.

Round 15: *(Joining Tail)* Sc in next st, ch 4; working on Tail, sc in each of next 8 sts; working in ch-4, sc in each of next 4 ch; working on Body, sl st in same st as first sc of round *(does not count as a st and is not worked into again)*, sc in each of next 23 sts on Body. (36 sc & 4 ch-sts) *(images 8 - 11)*

Round 16: Sc in next st; working in ch-4, sc in each of next 4 ch, sc in each of next 35 sts. (40 sc)

Rounds 17-18: *(2 rounds)* Sc in each st around. (40 sc)

Stuff Head and continue to stuff Body as you go.

Note: The triple crochet clusters in Round 19 will not be worked into again and are not included in overall stitch count.

Round 19: Sc in each of next 18 sts, skip next 2 sts, 8 trc in **front loop** of next st *(First Wing)*, skip next 2 sc; PM on each skipped st *(4 total)* and on unworked back loop behind First Wing; sc in each of next 12 sts, skip next 2 sts, 8 trc in **front loop** of next st *(Second Wing)*, skip next 2 sts; PM on each skipped st *(4 total)* and on unworked back loop behind Second Wing. (30 sc, 8 skipped sts & 2 unworked back loops) *(images 12 - 14)*

Round 20: Sc in each of next 7 sts, [dec] 2 times, sc in each of next 7 sts; removing markers as you encounter them, sc in each of next 2 skipped sts from previous round, sc in **back loop** behind First Wing, sc in each of next 2 skipped sts from previous round; sc in each of next 12 sts; removing markers as you encounter them, sc in each of next 2 skipped sts from previous round, sc in **back loop** behind Second Wing, sc in each of next 2 skipped sts from previous round. (38 sc) *(images 15 & 16)*

Round 21: Sc in each st around. (38 sc)

Note: In the next round, you will attach the Feet at their first attachment point, the marked unworked front loops (this will anchor them). When anchoring each Foot, hold the two marked unworked front loops on Round 2 of the foot against the next stitches on the Body with the back of the Foot (last row) directed upwards. Work the "attaching" stitches through the Foot and the Body together, across both layers.

Round 22: Sc in each of next 6 sts, dec, sc in each of next 2 sts, dec, sc in each of next 12 sts; *(Attach First Foot)* working on First Foot *(in marked front loops)* & Body, sc in each of next 2 sts; working on Body only, sc in each of next 4 sts; *(Attach Second Foot)* working on Second Foot *(in marked front loops)* & Body, sc in each of next 2 sts; working on Body only, sc in each of next 6 sts. (36 sc) *(images 17 - 19)*

Round 23: Sc in each st around. (36 sc)

Round 24: [Sc in each of next 4 sts, dec] 6 times. (30 sc)

Round 25: [Sc in each of next 3 sts, dec] 6 times. (24 sc)

Note: In the next round, you will attach the Feet at their second attachment point, the last row of each Foot. When attaching each Foot, flip the Foot up and hold the last row of the Foot against the next stitches on the Body. Work each "attaching" stitch through the Foot and the Body together, across both layers.

Round 26: Sc in each of next 14 sts; *(Attach First Foot)* working on First Foot *(in last Row)* & Body, sc in each of next 3 sts; working on Body only, sc in each of next 2 sts; *(Attach Second Foot)* working on Second Foot *(in last Row)* & Body, sc in each of next 3 sts; working on Body only, sc in each of next 2 sts. (24 sc) *(images 20 - 23)*

Round 27: [Sc in next st, dec] 8 times. (16 sc)

Round 28: [Dec] 8 times. (8 sc)

Fasten off, leaving a long tail for sewing.

1. Use yarn needle to weave yarn tail through front loops of final round and pull to close.

2. Add blush for cheeks.

FLOWER HAT

Petals (Make 5)

Round 1: With Color B, make a magic ring, (2 sc, hdc, dc, trc, dc, hdc, 2 sc) in ring. (4 sc, 2 hdc, 2 dc & 1 trc)

Round 2: Inc in each of next 2 sts, hdc-inc in next st, dc-inc in next st, 3 trc in next st, dc-inc in next st, hdc-inc in next st, inc in each of next 2 sts. (8 sc, 4 hdc, 4 dc & 3 trc)

Fasten off and weave in end.

Stem

Round 1: With Color C, make a magic ring, 5 sc in ring. (5 sc)

Round 2: Sc in each st around. (5 sc)

Round 3: Inc in each st around. (10 sc)

Note: In the next round, you will attach the Petals. When attaching each Petal, hold the central 2 sc-sts (within the group of 8 sc-sts) of the Petal against the next stitches on the Stem (you will only work into these 2 sts on the Petal; the remaining sts are left unworked) with the wrong side of the Petal facing outwards. Work the "attaching" stitches through the Petal and the Stem together, across both layers. The sides of the petals will overlap each other once attached.

Round 4: *(Attach Petals)* [Working on a Petal *(in central 2 sc-sts)* & Stem, sc in each of next 2 sts] 5 times. (40 sc) *(images 24 - 26)*

Fasten off and weave in end.

1. Place the Flower on the Duckling's Head.

AVRIL THE ELEPHANT

Avril was born at the circus. She travels the globe with her troop performing to crowds of admiring fans. Her speciality is walking the high wire and trapeze.

Skill Level: Advanced
Sewing Level: No-sew

Finished Size: 25 cm

Yarn:

Hobbii Honey Bunny (3.5 oz, 131 yds/100 g, 120 m)

Main Color (MC): Silver (118) for Legs, Arms, Trunk, Head & Body - 2 balls

Color A: Hint of Pink (50) for Legs & Cheeks - 1 ball

Color B: White (01) for Legs & Arms - 1 ball

Hobbii Honey Bunny Candy (3.5 oz, 131 yds/100 g, 120 m)

Color C: White (01) for Collar - 1 ball

Chenille yarn - your choice

Color D: An accent colour of your choice for Collar – small amount

Materials:

G-6 (4.00 mm) hook

Two 8 mm oval safety eyes

Stuffing

Stitch markers or scraps of yarn for marking stitches (19 required)

Yarn needle

Scissors

White fingering weight cotton yarn – small amount (ex. Hobbii Friends 8/4 Cotton)

Black embroidery floss

Ribbon or yarn for Collar - 12" (30 cm)

Orientation Check Points

Read these instructions carefully prior to starting the next round. You may be asked to alter the position of the start of the round before continuing.

Special Stitches:

Half Puff Stitch (½-puff)

Yarn over and insert your hook into the next stitch, yarn over and pull a loop through, yarn over and pull through 2 loops on your hook, yarn over and insert your hook back through the same stitch, yarn over and pull a loop through, yarn over and pull through 2 loops on your hook, yarn over and pull through all remaining loops on your hook.

LEG (Make 2)

Round 1: With Color A, make a magic ring, 8 sc in ring. (8 sc)

Round 2: Inc in each st around. (16 sc)

Change to MC.

Round 3: Sc in each of next 4 sts, inc in each of next 8 sts, sc in each of next 4 sts. (24 sc)

Round 4: Working in **back loops** only for entire round, sc in each of next 7 sts; [change to Color B, ½-puff in next st; change to MC, sc in each of next 2 sts] 3 times; change to Color B, ½-puff in next st; change to MC, sc in each of next 7 sts. (20 sc & 4 ½-puff-sts)

Rounds 5-6: *(2 rounds)* Sc in each st around. (24 sc)

Round 7: Sc in each of next 4 sts, [sc in each of next 2 sts, dec] 4 times, sc in each of next 4 sts. (20 sc)

Round 8: Sc in each st around. (20 sc)

Round 9: Sc in each of next 4 sts, [sc in next st, dec] 4 times, sc in each of next 4 sts. (16 sc)

Stuff Leg firmly.

Round 10: Sc in each st around. (16 sc)

Round 11: [Sc in each of next 2 sts, dec] 4 times. (12 sc)

Round 12: Sc in each st around. (12 sc)

Fasten off and weave in end. Alternatively, crochet over end when Leg attached to Body. *(image 1)*

ARM (Make 2)

Round 1: With MC, make a magic ring, 8 sc in ring. (8 sc)

Round 2: Inc in each st around. (16 sc)

Round 3: Working in **back loops** only for entire round, sc in each of next 5 sts; [change to Color B, ½-puff in next st, change to MC, sc in next st] 3 times, sc in each of next 5 sts. (13 sc & 3 ½-puff-sts)

Rounds 4-6: *(3 rounds)* Sc in each st around. (16 sc)

Round 7: [Sc in each of next 2 sts, dec] 4 times. (12 sc)

Rounds 8-10: *(3 rounds)* Sc in each st around. (12 sc)

Stuff lower 2/3 of Arm.

Round 11: [Sc in next st, dec] 4 times. (8 sc)

Orientation Check Point
Flatten the top of the Arm so that the middle ½-puff stitch is in line with one side of the flattened end (the row of ½-puff stitches is perpendicular to the flattened end). You want the end of round to be to one side of the flattened end. If needed, work additional single crochet stitches to move the end of round to the side of the Arm.

Closing Row: Flatten Arm, ch 1; working through both layers *(to close opening)*, sc in each of next 4 sts. (4 sc)

Fasten off and weave in end. Alternatively, crochet over end when Arm attached to Body. *(image 2)*

UPPER TRUNK

Note: Each section of the Trunk & Head has been made in a contrasting color in the photos for clarity.

Round 1: With MC, make a magic ring, 8 sc in ring; PM on **back loop** of first st of round. (8 sc)

Round 2: Working in **font loops** only, sl st in each st around *(these sts will not be worked into again)*. (8 sl st)

Remove your hook from the working loop, insert your hook into the next sl st from inside to outside, then place the working loop back on your hook and pull it through to the inside of the piece. *(image 3)*

Round 3: Working in unworked **back loops** of Round 1 only, sc in each st around. (8 sc)

Fasten off and weave in end. *(image 4)*

LOWER TRUNK

Round 1: With MC, ch 4; inc in 2nd ch from hook, sc in next ch, 4 sc in last ch; working on other side of starting ch, sc in next ch, inc in last ch. (10 sc)

Round 2: Inc in each of next 2 sts, sc in next st, inc in each of next 4 sts, sc in next st, inc in each of next 2 sts. (18 sc)

Round 3: [Sc in next st, inc in next st] 2 times, sc in next st, [inc in next st, sc in next st] 2 times, [sc in next st, inc in next st] 2 times, sc in next st, [inc in next st, sc in next st] 2 times. (26 sc)

Round 4: Sc in each of next 2 sts, inc in next st, sc in each of next 7 sts, inc in next st, sc in each of next 4 sts, inc in next st, sc in each of next 7 sts, inc in next st, sc in each of next 2 sts. (30 sc)

Round 5: Sc in each of next 29 sts; leave last st unworked. (30 sc) *(image 5)*

Note: In the next round you will attach the Upper Trunk to the Lower Trunk. When attaching the Upper Trunk, hold any two stitches in the last round of the Upper Trunk against the next stitches on the Lower Trunk with Round 1 of the Upper Truck pointing downwards. Work the "attaching" stitches through the Upper Trunk (from inside to outside) and Lower Trunk together, across both layers. Attaching stitches will not be worked into again and are not included in overall stitch count. When starting the round, continue from where you left off from Round 5. Your start of Round will change (the new start of round is noted within Round 6).

Round 6: *(Attach Upper Trunk)* Working on Upper Trunk & Lower Trunk, sc in each of next 2 sts; PM on each attaching st; *(next st is new start of round)* working on Lower Trunk only, sc in each of next 5 sts, insert hook in next st, skip next 16 sts, insert hook from inside to outside in next st and sl st across both layers *(sl st will not be worked into again and will not be included in overall st count)*; sc in each of next 4 sts; insert hook from inside to outside through next st and then from outside to inside through same stitch in Upper Trunk as first attaching stitch of round and sc across both layers *(see photo; this step prevents gaps)*; working on unworked sts of Upper Trunk, sc in each of next 6 sts. (16 sc) *(images 6 - 9)*

Round 7: Insert hook from inside to outside through same stitch in Upper Trunk as second attaching stitch of Round 6 and then from outside to inside through next st on Lower Trunk and make a sc across both layers; working on Lower Trunk, sc in each of next 5 sts, insert hook in same st as last st, skip 16 skipped sts and sl st from previous round, insert hook from inside to outside in next st and sc across both layers, sc in each of next 9 sts. (16 sc) *(images 10 - 12)*

Remove stitch markers on attaching stitches. Stuff Upper Trunk.

Round 8: [Dec] 8 times. (8 sc)

Fasten off, leaving a long tail for sewing. Use yarn needle to weave yarn tail through front loops of final round and pull to close.

LOWER TRUNK & HEAD

Note: You will now work into the 16 unworked stitches of the Lower Trunk. (image 13)

Round 1: Attach MC to 9th unworked st on Lower Trunk *(see photo)*, sc in same st, sc in each of next 7 sts, insert hook in same st as last st, skip next sl st, insert hook from inside to outside in next st and sc across both layers, sc in each of next 7 sts. (16 sc)

Round 2: Sc in each st around. (16 sc)

Stuff lower part of Trunk.

Round 3: Sc in each of next 4 sts, hdc-inc in each of next 8 sts, sc in each of next 4 sts. (8 sc & 16 hdc) PM on 2 middle hdc-sts *(shown in yellow in photo; marks center of Head and will help with orientation)*. *(image 14)*

Round 4: Sc in each of next 4 sts, [sc in next st, inc in next st] 4 times, [inc in next st, sc in next st] 4 times, sc in each of next 4 sts. (32 sc)

Note: In the next round, you will anchor the Trunk to the Head, working through the side of the Trunk closest to the Head. When anchoring the Trunk, hold the side of the Trunk (near the Trunk's closing round) against the next stitches on the Head. Work each "attaching" stitch through the two closest stitch holes on the Trunk (inside then outside) and into the next stitch on the Head together, across both layers.

Round 5: Sc in each of next 4 sts, [inc in next st, sc in each of next 2 sts] 3 times, inc in next st, sc in next st; *(Attach Trunk)* working on Trunk & Head, sc in each of next 2 sts; working on Head only, sc in next st, inc in next st, [sc in each of next 2 sts, inc in next st] 3 times, sc in each of next 4 sts. (40 sc) *(images 15 - 17)*

Rounds 6-8: *(3 rounds)* Sc in each of next 40 sts. (40 sc)

> **Orientation Check Point**
> The next round should start centrally at the base of the Head (directly opposite the marked central hdc-sts in Round 3). If needed, move the start of round forward (by making additional single crochet stitches), or back (by removing single crochet stitches) to allow for this. To mark the center of each Ear for the next round, place markers on the **back loops** of the 10th and 31st stitches of Round 8 (see photo).

Note: The ears are a bit tricky. Take your time. Mark stitches where instructed; they will help you identify stitches you will need to work into during the following round. The stitches that make up the Ears are not included in overall stitch count. At the end of Round 9, you will start to make the opening for the Body. (image 18)

Round 9: Sc in each of next 8 sts; do not fasten off; continue to First Ear, working in rows.

First Ear

Row 1: Skip next st; PM on skipped st, 8 dc in **front loop** of next st *(this should be in front of stitch marker indicating center of Ear)*, skip next st; PM on skipped st; sl st in **front loop** of next st; PM on unworked **back loop** of same st; ch 2, skip next st; PM on skipped st; sl st in **front loop** of next st; PM on unworked **back loop** of same st. *(images 19 - 21)*

Row 2: Turn; skipping to dc-sts from Row 1, dc-inc in each of next 8 dc, skip next st *(on Head)*; PM on skipped st; sl st in **back loop** of next st *(on Head)*; PM on unworked **front loop** of same st. *(image 22)*

Row 3: Turn; ch 2; skipping to dc-sts from Row 2, dc-inc in each of next 5 dc, hdc-inc in each of next 2 dc, hdc in each of next 2 dc, sc in each of next 4 dc, slst in each of next 3 dc. Do not fasten off. Continue on Head. *(image 23)*

Round 9 continued: Working on Head, sc in each of next 15 sts; do not fasten off, continue to Second Ear, working in rows.

Second Ear

Rows 1-2: *(2 rows)* Repeat Rows 1-2 of First Ear.

Row 3: Turn, ch 1; skipping to dc-sts from Row 2, sl st in each of next 3 dc, sc in each of next 4 dc, hdc in each of next 2 dc, hdc-inc in each of next 2 dc, dc-inc in each of next 5 dc, ch 2, sl st in same st. Do not fasten off. Continue on Head.

Round 9 continued: Working on Head, sc in each of next 2 sts, ch 6, skip last 3 sts.

*Note: At the start of the next round, you will complete the opening for the Body. You will also be working into the marked unworked loops (in **back loop** only) and skipped stitches (in both loops) behind each Ear. Fold the Ears downwards onto the face as you work behind them.*

Round 10: Skip next 3 sts *(Body opening)*, sc in each of next 2 sts; move start of round marker to 4th ch of ch-6 from Round 9; sc through inner edge of First Ear and next st on Head together across both layers; working behind First Ear and removing markers as you encounter them, sc in each of next 8 marked sts; working on Head, sc in each of next 12 sts; sc through inner edge of Second Ear and next st on Head together across both layers; working behind Second Ear and removing markers as you encounter them, sc in each of next 8 marked sts; working on Head, sc in each of next 2 sts; working in ch-6, sc in each of next 3 ch. (37 sc & 3 ch-sts) *(images 24 & 25)*

Do not fasten off.

Face Details

1. Insert your safety eyes between Rounds 5 & 6 on either side of Trunk.

2. With Color A, embroider small Cheeks on the lower outer aspects of the Eyes.

3. With white fingering weight cotton yarn, embroider small highlights on outer aspects of safety eyes (optional).

4. With black embroidery floss, embroider small Eyebrows 2 rounds above the eyes.

Continue with Head.

Round 11: Working in ch-6, sc in each of next 3 ch, sc in each remaining st around. (40 sc)

Rounds 12-13: *(2 rounds)* Sc in each st around. (40 sc)

Stuff Head.

Round 14: [Sc in each of next 3 sts, dec] 8 times. (32 sc)

Round 15: [Sc in each of next 2 sts, dec] 8 times. (24 sc)

Round 16: [Sc in next st, dec] 8 times. (16 sc)

Round 17: [Dec] 8 times. (8 sc)

Fasten off, leaving a long tail for sewing. Use yarn needle to weave yarn tail through front loops of final round and pull to close. *(image 26)*

BODY

Note: In the next round, you will be working around the Body opening made in Rounds 9 and 10 of the Head, starting in the ch-6.

The stitch markers in the photo mark the corner spaces of Body opening. (images 27 & 28)

Round 1: Attach MC at center back of Body opening (3 ch-sts away from next corner space), sc in same ch, sc in each of next 2 ch, inc in next corner space between rounds, sc in each of next 6 sts, inc in next corner space between rounds, sc in each of next 3 ch. (16 sc)

Round 2: [Sc in next st, inc in next st] 8 times. (24 sc)

Note: In the next round, you will attach the Arms. When attaching each Arm, hold the closing stitches of the Arm against the next stitches on the Body with the Arm ½-puff stitches facing the same direction as the Elephant's Face. Work the "attaching" stitches through the Arm and the Body together, across both layers.

Round 3: Sc in each of next 4 sts; *(Attach First Arm)* working on First Arm & Body, sc in each of next 4 sts; working on Body only, sc in each of next 8 sts; *(Attach Second Arm)* working on Second Arm & Body, sc in each of next 4 sts; working on Body only, sc in each of next 4 sts. (24 sc) *(images 29 & 30)*

Round 4: [Sc in each of next 2 sts, inc in next st] 8 times. (32 sc)

Rounds 5-6: *(2 rounds)* Sc in each st around. (32 sc)

Round 7: [Sc in each of next 3 sts, inc in next st] 8 times. (40 sc)

Rounds 8-13: *(6 rounds)* Sc in each st around. (40 sc)

Orientation Check Point

The next round should start centrally at the back of the Body. If needed, move the start of round forward (by making additional single crochet stitches), or back (by removing single crochet stitches) to allow for this.

Note: In the next round, you will attach the Legs. The position of each Leg has been mapped out with green and blue stitch markers in the photo. When attaching each Leg, hold the 6 sts at the front of the Leg (you will only work into these front 6 sts; the remaining sts are left unworked this round) against the next stitches on the Body with the ½-puff stitches pointing towards the Body. Work the "attaching" stitches through the Leg (from inside to outside) and the Body together, across both layers. (image 31)

Round 14: Sc in each of next 11 sts; *(Attach First Leg)* working on First Leg *(in front 6 sts)* & Body, sc in each of next 6 sts; PMs on 1st and 6th attaching sts; working on Body only, sc in each of next 6 sts; *(Attach Second Leg)* working on Second Leg *(in front 6 sts)* & Body, sc in each of next 6 sts; PMs on 1st and 6th attaching sts; working on Body only, sc in each of next 11 sts. (40 sc) *(images 32 & 33)*

Note: In the next round, you will crochet into the unworked stitches of each Leg. The attaching stitches from the previous round are not worked into again and are not included in overall stitch count.

Round 15: Sc in each of next 10 sts, insert hook from inside to outside through next st on Body and then from outside to inside through same stitch in First Leg as first marked attaching stitch and sc across both layers; working on First Leg, sc in each of next 6 sts, insert hook from inside to outside through same stitch in First Leg as second marked attaching stitch and then from outside to inside through next st on Body and sc across both layers; working on Body, sc in each of next 4 sts, insert hook from inside to outside through next st on Body and then from outside to inside through same stitch in Second Leg as first marked attaching stitch and sc across both layers; working on Second Leg, sc in each of next 6 sts, insert hook from inside to outside through same stitch in Second Leg as second marked attaching stitch and then from outside to inside through next st on Body and sc across both layers; working on Body, sc in each of next 10 sts. (40 sc) *(images 34 -38)*

Stuff Body and Legs firmly and continue to stuff as you go. Remove stitch markers from Legs.

Note: In the next round, you will make the Tail. The stitches of the Tail will not be included in overall stitch count.

Round 16: Sc in next st, ch 13, sl st in 7th ch from hook, [ch 6, sl st back into 7th ch of ch-13] 2 times; working in ch-13, sl st in each of next 6 ch, sl st in **front loop** of first sc of round , sc in each of next 2 sts, dec, [sc in each of next 3 sts, dec] 7 times. (32 sc) *(image 39)*

Round 17: Fold Tail towards you so that it remains on outside of Body; sc in unworked **back loop** of next st, sc in next st, dec, [sc in each of next 2 sts, dec] 7 times (24 sc)

Round 18: [Sc in next st, dec] 8 times. (16 sc)

Round 19: [Dec] 8 times. (8 sc)

Fasten off, leaving a long tail for sewing. Use yarn needle to weave yarn tail through front loops of final round and pull to close.

COLLAR

Row 1: With Color D, ch 19; sc in 2nd ch from hook, sc in each of next 17 ch. (18 sc)

Row 2: Ch 1, turn, inc in each st across. (36 sc)

Change to Color C.

Row 3: Ch 2, turn, hdc-inc in each st across. (72 hdc)

Change to Color D.

Row 4: Turn, sl st in each st across. (72 sl sts)

Fasten off and weave in ends.

1. Thread ribbon through one end of Collar at Row 1.

2. Wrap Collar around Elephant's Neck and thread the ribbon through the other end of Collar.

3. Tie ribbon in a bow to secure.

FOGARTY THE FOX

Fogarty is incredibly smart and cunning. She spends her nights at the Bodleian library reading everything she can get her paws on. She dreams of being the first fox professor at Oxford University.

Skill Level: Intermediate
Sewing Level: Low-sew

Finished Size: 26 cm

Yarn:

Hobbii Honey Bunny (3.5 oz, 131 yds/100 g, 120 m)

Main Color (MC): Gold Dust (27) for Nose, Ears, Tail, Front Legs & Body - 1 ball

Color A: White (01) for Nose, Head, Tail & Body - 1 ball

Color B: Chocolate (12) for Nose, Ears, Back Legs & Front Legs - 1 ball

Color C: Hint of Pink (50) for Back Legs & Front Legs - small amount

Materials:

G-6 (4.00 mm) hook

Two 25 mm kawaii sinker safety eyes (alternatively, use 15 mm black safety eyes with a 25 mm diameter circle of colored felt behind)

Stuffing

Stitch markers

Yarn needle

Scissors

White fingering weight cotton yarn (ex. Hobbii Rainbow Cotton 8/4)

Foam roller (optional)

Orientation Check Points

Read these instructions carefully prior to starting the next round. You may be asked to alter the position of the start of the round before continuing.

NOSE

Round 1: With Color B, make a magic ring, 6 sc in ring. (6 sc) Change to Color A.

Round 2: Working in **back loops** only, sc in each of next 3 sts; change to MC; working in **back loops** only, sc in each of next 3 sts. (6 sc)

Change to Color A.

Round 3: Sc in next st, inc in next st, sc in next st; change to MC, inc in next st, sc in next st, inc in next st. (9 sc)

Change to Color A.

Round 4: Inc in next st, sc in each of next 2 sts, inc in next st; change to MC, hdc in each of next 2 sts, hdc-inc in next st, hdc in each of next 2 sts. (6 sc & 6 hdc)

Fasten off and weave in end. *(image 1)*

EARS

First Ear

Round 1: With Color B, make a magic ring, 4 sc in ring. (4 sc)

Round 2: [Inc in next st, sc in next st] 2 times. (6 sc)

Round 3: [Inc in next st, sc in each of next 2 sts] 2 times. (8 sc)

Round 4: [Inc in next st, sc in each of next 3 sts] 2 times. (10 sc)

Round 5: [Inc in next st, sc in each of next 4 sts] 2 times. (12 sc) Change to MC.

Round 6: [Inc in next st, sc in each of next 5 sts] 2 times. (14 sc) Do not stuff. Fasten off.

Second Ear

Rounds 1-6: *(6 rounds)* Repeat Rounds 1-6 of First Ear.

Do not stuff. Do not fasten off. Continue with Head.

HEAD

Round 7: *(Joining Ears)* From Second Ear, ch 4; working on First Ear, sc in next st; move start of round to st just made; sc in each of next 13 sts on First Ear; working in ch-4, sc in next ch, inc in each of next 2 ch, sc in last ch; working on Second Ear, sc in each of next 14 sts; working on other side of ch-4, sc in next ch, inc in each of next 2 ch, sc in last ch. (40 sc) *(images 2 - 6)*

Round 8: Sc in each of next 14 sts, inc in next st, sc in each of next 4 sts, inc in next st, sc in each of next 14 sts, inc in next st, sc in each of next 4 sts, inc in next st. (44 sc)

Round 9: Sc in each of next 6 sts, inc in each of next 2 sts, sc in each of next 20 sts, inc in each of next 2 sts, sc in each of next 14 sts. (48 sc)

Rounds 10-11: *(2 rounds)* Sc in each st around. (48 sc)

Orientation Check Point
The next round should start centrally at the back of the Head. If needed, move the start of round forward (by making additional single crochet stitches), or back (by removing single crochet stitches) to allow for this.

Round 12: Sc in each of next 4 sts, [sc in each of next 3 sts, inc in next st] 4 times, sc in each of next 8 sts, [inc in next st, sc in each of next 3 sts] 4 times, sc in each of next 4 sts. (56 sc)

Rounds 13-14: *(2 rounds)* Sc in each st around. (56 sc)

Orientation Check Point
In the next round, you will start to attach the nose. The round should start centrally at the back of the Head. If needed, move the start of round forward (by making additional single crochet stitches), or back (by removing single crochet stitches) to allow for this.

Note: When attaching the Nose, hold the Nose upside down with the 6 sts in MC (you will only work into these 6 sts; the remaining sts are left unworked this round) against the next stitches on the Head. Work the "attaching" stitches through the Nose (from inside to outside) and the Head together, across both layers. *(image 7)*

Round 15: Sc in each of next 4 sts, [sc in each of next 4 sts, inc in next st] 4 times, sc in next st; *(Attach Nose)* working on Nose *(in 6 MC sts)* & Head, sc in each of next 6 sts ; working on Head only, sc in next st, [inc in next st, sc in each of next 4 sts] 4 times, sc in each of next 4 sts. (64 sc) *(images 8 & 9)*

Note: In the next round, you will crochet into the unworked Color A stitches of the Nose. The MC attaching stitches of the Nose from the previous round will not be worked into again and are not included in overall stitch count.

Change to Color A.

Round 16: Sc in each of next 29 sts; working on Nose, inc in next st, sc in each of next 4 sts, inc in next st; working on Head sc in each of next 29 sts. (66 sc) *(images 10 - 12)*

Round 17: Sc in each of next 29 sts, dec, sc in each of next 4 sts, dec, sc in each of next 29 sts. (64 sc)

Rounds 18-20: *(3 rounds)* Sc in each st around. (64 sc)

Insert safety eyes between Rounds 15 & 16 on either side Nose. *(image 13)*

Stuff Head and continue to stuff as your go.

Orientation Check Point
In the next round, you will start decreasing. The round should start centrally at the back of the Head. If needed, move the start of round forward (by making additional single crochet stitches), or back (by removing single crochet stitches) to allow for this.

Round 21: Sc in each of next 4 sts, [sc in each of next 4 sts, dec] 4 times, sc in each of next 8 sts, [dec, sc in each of next 4 sts] 4 times, sc in each of next 4 sts. (56 sc)

Round 22: Sc in each of next 4 sts, [sc in each of next 3 sts, dec] 4 times, sc in each of next 8 sts, [dec, sc in each of next 3 sts] 4 times, sc in each of next 4 sts. (48 sc)

Round 23: Sc in each of next 4 sts, [sc in each of next 2 sts, dec] 4 times, sc in each of next 8 sts, [dec, sc in each of next 2 sts] 4 times, sc in each of next 4 sts. (40 sc)

Round 24: Sc in each of next 4 sts, [sc in next st, dec] 4 times, sc in each of next 8 sts, [dec, sc in next st] 4 times, sc in each of next 4 sts. (32 sc)

Round 25: Sc in each of next 4 sts, [dec] 4 times, sc in each of next 8 sts, [dec] 4 times, sc in each of next 4 sts. (24 sc)

Round 26: Sc in each of next 2 sts, [dec, sc in next st] 2 times, dec, sc in each of next 4 sts, [dec, sc in next st] 2 times, dec, sc in each of next 2 sts. (18 sc)

Fasten off and weave in end. *(image 14)*

TAIL

Round 1: With Color A, make a magic ring, 4 sc in ring. (4 sc)

Round 2: [Inc in next st, sc in next st] 2 times. (6 sc)

Round 3: [Inc in next st, sc in each of next 2 sts] 2 times. (8 sc)

Round 4: [Inc in next st, sc in each of next 3 sts] 2 times. (10 sc)

Round 5: [Inc in next st, sc in each of next 4 sts] 2 times. (12 sc)

Change to MC.

Round 6: Sc in each st around. (12 sc)

Round 7: [Sc in next st, inc in next st] 6 times. (18 sc)

Rounds 8-11: *(4 rounds)* Sc in each st around. (18 sc)

Stuff Tail and continue to stuff as you go.

Round 12: Working in **back loops** only, sc in next st, dec; PM on each of first two unworked front loops; working in both loops, [sc in next st, dec] 5 times. (12 sc)

Round 13: [Sc in next st, dec] 4 times. (8 sc)

Rounds 14-19: *(6 rounds)* Sc in each st around. (8 sc) Stuff these rounds very lightly.

> **Orientation Check Point**
> Flatten the top of the Tail so that the marked unworked front loops both face upwards, parallel to the flattened end. You want the end of round to be to one side of the flattened end. If needed, work additional single crochet stitches to move the end of round to the side of the Tail.

Closing Row: Flatten Tail, ch 1; working through both layers *(to close opening)*, sc in each of next 4 sts. (4 sc)

Fasten off. *(image 15)*

BACK LEG (Make 2)

Round 1: With Color C, make a magic ring, 8 sc in ring. (8 sc)

Round 2: Inc in each st around. (16 sc)

Change to Color B.

Round 3: Sc in each of next 4 sts, inc in each of next 8 sts, sc in each of next 4 sts. (24 sc)

Rounds 4-5: *(2 rounds)* Sc in each st around. (24 sc)

Round 6: Sc in each of next 4 sts, [sc in each of next 2 sts, dec] 4 times, sc in each of next 4 sts. (20 sc)

Round 7: Sc in each of next 4 sts, [sc in next st, dec] 4 times, sc in each of next 4 sts. (16 sc)

Round 8: Sc in each of next 2 sts, [dec, sc in next st] 4 times, sc in each of next 2 sts. (12 sc)

Round 9: Sc in each of next 2 sts, [dec] 4 times, sc in next st; leave remaining st unworked. (8 sc)

Stuff Back Leg

Closing Row: Flatten Back Leg, ch 1; working through both layers *(to close opening)*, sc in each of next 4 sts. (4 sc)

Fasten off. *(image 16)*

FRONT LEG (Make 2)

Round 1: With Color C, make a magic ring, 8 sc in ring. (8 sc)

Change to Color B.

Round 2: Inc in each st around. (16 sc)

Round 3: Working in **back loops** only, sc in each st around. (16 sc)

Rounds 4-5: *(2 rounds)* Sc in each st around. (16 sc)

Round 6: Sc in each of next 4 sts, [dec] 4 times, sc in each of next 4 sts. (12 sc)

Change to MC.

Stuff Front Leg and continue to stuff as you go. Gradually decrease volume of stuffing towards end of Leg.

Rounds 7-15: *(9 rounds)* Sc in each st around. (12 sc)

Fasten off and weave in end. *(image 17)*

BODY

Round 1: With MC, make a magic ring, 8 sc in ring. (8 sc)

Round 2: Inc in each st around. (16 sc)

Round 3: Sc in each of next 4 sts, inc in each of next 4 sts, sc in each of next 4 sts, inc in each of next 4 sts. (24 sc)

Round 4: Sc in each of next 4 sts, [sc in next st, inc in next st] 4 times, sc in each of next 4 sts, [sc in next st, inc in next st] 4 times. (32 sc)

Round 5: Sc in each of next 4 sts, [sc in each of next 2 sts, inc in next st] 4 times, sc in each of next 4 sts, [sc in each of next 2 sts, inc in next st] 4 times. (40 sc)

Note: In the next round, you will attach the Tail and Back Legs. When attaching the Tail, hold the closing stitches of the Tail against the next stitches on the Body with the Tail stitch markers facing outwards. When attaching each Back Leg, hold the closing stitches of the Back Leg against the next stitches on the Body with the foot pointing outwards. Work the "attaching" stitches through the Tail or Back Leg and the Body together, across both layers. (images 18 - 21)

Round 6: (Attach Tail) Working on Tail & Body, sc in each of next 4 sts; working on Body only, sc in each of next 10 sts; (Attach First Back Leg) working on First Back Leg & Body, sc in each of next 4 sts; working on Body only, sc in each of next 8 sts; (Attach Second Back Leg) working on Second Back Leg & Body, sc in each of next 4 sts; working on Body only, sc in each of next 10 sts. (40 sc) *(image 22)*

Rounds 7-11: *(5 rounds)* Sc in each st around. (40 sc)

Note: In the next round, you will anchor the Tail to the body, through the marked unworked front loops of the Tail. When anchoring the Tail, hold the two marked front loops on Round 17 of the Tail against the next stitches on the Body. Work the "attaching" stitches through the Tail and the Body together, across both layers.

Round 12: Sc in each of next 2 sts; *(Attach Tail)* working on Tail *(in marked front loops)* & Body, sc in each of next 2 sts; working on Body only, sc in each of next 36 sts. (40 sc) *(images 23 - 25)*

Orientation Check Point
Make an additional single crochet stitch and move the start of round forward by one stitch.

Round 13: Sc in each of next 4 sts, [sc in each of next 2 sts, dec] 4 times, sc in each of next 4 sts, [sc in each of next 2 sts, dec] 4 times. (32 sc)

Rounds 14-15: *(2 rounds)* Sc in each st around. (32 sc)

Stuff Body and continue to stuff as your go.

Note: In the next round, you will attach the Front Legs. When attaching each Front Leg, hold the 4 sts at the back of the Leg (you will only work into these back 4 sts; the remaining sts are left unworked this round) against the next stitches on the Body with the foot pointing outwards. Work the "attaching" stitches through the Front Leg (from inside to outside) and the Body together, across both layers.

Round 16: Sc in each of next 14 sts; *(Attach First Front Leg)* working on First Front Leg *(in back 4 sts)* & Body, sc in each of next 4 sts *(tthese sts are marked with stitch markers in the photos)*; change to Color A; working on Body only, sc in each of next 2 sts; change to MC; *(Attach Second Front Leg)* working on Second Front Leg *(in back 4 sts)* & Body, sc in each of next 4 sts; working on Body only, sc in each of next 8 sts. (32 sc) *(images 26 - 29)*

Note: In the next round, you will crochet into the unworked stitches of each Front Leg. The attaching stitches of the Legs from the previous round (as shown in Color B in photos) will not be worked into again and are not included in overall stitch count.

Round 17: Sc in each of next 6 sts, dec, sc in each of next 4 sts, dec; working on First Front Leg, sc in next st, dec, sc in each of next 2 sts, dec, sc in next st; change to Color A; working on Body, sc in each of next 2 sts: change to MC; working on Second Front Leg, sc in next st, dec, sc in each of next 2 sts, dec, sc in next st; working on Body, dec, sc in each of next 4 sts, dec. (32 sc) *(images 30 -32)*

Round 18: Sc in each of next 17 sts; change to Color A, sc in each of next 4 sts; change to MC, sc in each of next 11 sts. (32 sc)

Round 19: [Sc in each of next 2 sts, dec] 2 times; change to Color A, [sc in each of next 2 sts, dec] 5 times, sc in each of next 2 sts; change to MC, dec. (24 sc)

Round 20: Sc in each of next 3 sts; change to Color A, sc in each of next 21 sts. (24 sc)

Round 21: [Sc in each of next 2 sts, dec] 6 times. (18 sc)

Fasten off and weave in end. *(image 33)*

ASSEMBLY

1. Using white fingering weight cotton yarn, sew the Head to the Body. Ensure there is adequate stuffing around the neck prior to closing to prevent the Head from being floppy. Alternatively, foam rollers may be added to reinforce the Neck. *(images 34 & 35)*

GARDEN FRIENDS

Pappa Mushie loves to tend his vegetable patch. His neighbour, Lucy the Snail, shares his passion for gardening. They talk for hours daily on the subject; however, they still cannot agree on the best way to grow tomatoes.

Skill Level: Intermediate
Sewing Level: Low-sew

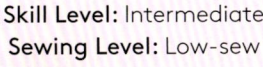

Finished Size:
Mushroom 28 cm & Snail 17 cm

Yarn:

Hobbii Honey Bunny (3.5 oz, 131 yds/100 g, 120 m)

Main Color 1 (MC-1): Oatmilk (03) for Body & Head of Snail - 1 ball

Color A: Mulberry (55) for Shell of Snail & Cap of Mushroom - 1 ball

Hobbii Toucan (3.5 oz, 131 yds/100 g, 120 m)

Main Color 2 (MC-2): Ecru (02) for Body & Flowers of Mushroom - 1 ball

Color B: Sage (28) for Scarf of Snail – small amount

Materials:

G-6 (4.00 mm) hook
Two 8 mm oval safety eyes per toy
Stuffing
Stitch markers
Yarn needle

Scissors
Black embroidery floss
Blush (optional)
Toy glasses for mushroom (optional)

Orientation Check Points
Read these instructions carefully prior to starting the next round. You may be asked to alter the position of the start of the round before continuing.

MUSHROOM

BODY

Round 1: With MC-2, make a magic ring, 8 sc in ring. (8 sc)

Round 2: Inc in each st around. (16 sc)

Round 3: [Sc in next st, inc in next st] 8 times. (24 sc)

Round 4: [Sc in each of next 2 sts, inc in next st] 8 times. (32 sc)

Rounds 5-8: *(4 rounds)* Sc in each st around. (32 sc)

Round 9: [Sc in each of next 6 sts, dec] 4 times. (28 sc)

Rounds 10-11: *(2 rounds)* Sc in each st around. (28 sc)

Round 12: [Sc in each of next 5 sts, dec] 4 times. (24 sc)

Round 13: Working in **back loops** only, sc in each of next 11 sts, puff in next st, sc in each of next 12 sts. (23 sc & 1 puff) PM on first st of this round. *(image 1)*

Round 14: Working in unworked **front loops** of Round 12 only *(in front of Round 13)*, sl st in each of next 5 sts, inc in next st, hdc-inc in each of next 2 sts, dc-inc in next st, hdc in next st, sc in next st, sl st in next st, sc in next st, hdc in next st, dc-inc in next st, hdc-inc in each of next 2 sts, inc in next st, sl st in each of next 6 sts. (32 sts) *(images 2 & 3)*

Note: The stitches made in Round 14 will not be worked in again. Return to Round 13 and continue by working into the stitches of Round 13 (start at marker placed in first stitch of Round 13).

Round 15: Sc in each st around. (24 sc)

Round 16: [Sc in each of next 2 sts, dec] 6 times. (18 sc)

Place safety eyes in Round 15 on either side of puff stitch from Round 13.

Rounds 17-19: *(3 rounds)* Sc in each st around. (18 sc)

Start to stuff Body and continue to stuff as you go.

Round 20: Working in **front loops** only, [sl st in next st, PICOT, sl st in next st] 9 times. (18 sl sts & 9 PICOT) *(image 4)*

Note: The stitches made in Round 20 will not be worked into again.

Round 21: Working in unworked **back loops** of Round 19 only *(behind Round 20)*, sc in each st around. (18 sc)

Rounds 22-23: *(2 rounds)* Sc in each st around. (18 sc)

Round 24: Working in **front loops** only, inc in each st around. (36 sc)

Round 25: [FPsc in next st, sc in each of next 4 sts, inc in next st] 6 times. (42 sts) *(images 5 & 6)*

Round 26: [FPsc in next st, sc in each of next 5 sts, inc in next st] 6 times. (48 sts)

Round 27: [FPsc in next st, sc in each of next 6 sts, inc in next st] 6 times. (54 sts)

Round 28: [FPsc in next st, sc in each of next 7 sts, inc in next st] 6 times. (60 sts)

Round 29: [FPsc in next st, sc in each of next 8 sts, inc in next st] 6 times. (66 sts)

Fasten off and weave in end.

Face Details

1. With black embroidery floss, embroider eyebrows on the upper outer aspects of the safety eyes.

2. Use blush to add Cheeks (optional).

MUSHROOM CAP

Round 1: With Color A, make a magic ring, 6 sc in ring. (6 sc)

Round 2: Inc in each st around. (12 sc)

Round 3: [Sc in next st, inc in next st] 6 times. (18 sc)

Round 4: Sc in each st around. (18 sc)

Round 5: [Sc in each of next 2 sts, inc in next st] 6 times. (24 sc)

Round 6: Sc in each st around. (24 sc)

Round 7: [Sc in each of next 3 sts, inc in next st] 6 times. (30 sc)

Round 8: Sc in each st around. (30 sc)

Round 9: [Sc in each of next 4 sts, inc in next st] 6 times. (36 sc)

Round 10: Sc in each st around. (36 sc)

Round 11: [Sc in each of next 5 sts, inc in next st] 6 times. (42 sc)

Round 12: [Sc in each of next 6 sts, inc in next st] 6 times. (48 sc)

Round 13: Sc in each st around. (48 sc)

Round 14: [Sc in each of next 7 sts, inc in next st] 6 times. (54 sc)

Round 15: [Sc in each of next 8 sts, inc in next st] 6 times. (60 sc)

Round 16: [Sc in each of next 9 sts, inc in next st] 6 times. (66 sc) Stuff Cap lightly. *(image 7)*

Note: In the next round you will attach the Body to the Cap. With the wrong side of each piece facing each other, place the Body in the Cap, lining up the stitches of the last round of the Body with the stitches of Round 16 of the Cap. Work the "attaching" stitches through the Cap and then the Body together, across both layers.

Round 17: *(Attach Body)* Working on Cap & Body, sc in each st around. (66 sc)

Round 18: [Sc in each of next 10 sts, inc in next st] 6 times. (72 sc) Fasten off and weave in end.

Flowers: With MC-2, embroider flowers on Mushroom Cap (optional). *(image 8)*

SNAIL

SHELL

Note: The shell will be formed into a spiral and crocheted together as you go.

Round 1: With Color A, ch 6, sc in 2nd ch from hook, sc in each of next 3 ch, 3 sc in last ch; working on other side of starting ch, sc in each of next 3 ch, inc in last ch. (12 sc)

Round 2: Sc in each st around. (12 sc)

Round 3: Working in **back loops** only, sc in each st around. (12 sc)

Round 4: Sc in each st around. (12 sc)

Round 5: Working in **back loops** only, sc in each st around. (12 sc)

Add a little stuffing. This stuffed section will become the center of the Shell once it is rolled into a spiral. Do not stuff remainder of Shell.

Note: In the next round, you will attach the unworked front loops of a previous round to the current round to create a spiral. When attaching the unworked front loops, roll the Shell tightly until they are against the next stitches on the current round. Work the "attaching" stitches through the previous round (in the unworked front loops) and the current round together, across both layers.

Round 6: Sc in each of next 7 sts; roll Shell so unworked front loops of Round 3 line up with next stitches on current round; working on unworked front loops & current round, sc in each of next 4 sts; working on current round only, sc in next st. (12 sc) *(image 9)*

Round 7: Working in **back loops** only, sc in each st around. (12 sc)

Round 8: Sc in each st around. (12 sc)

Round 9: Working in **back loops** only, sc in each st around. (12 sc)

Round 10: Sc in each st around. (12 sc)

Round 11: Working in **back loops** only, sc in each st around. (12 sc)

Note: In Rounds 12, 16, 20, 24, 28, 32, 36 & 40, you will attach unworked front loops of a previous round to the current round. Use the same method as Round 6 of the Shell.

Round 12: Sc in each of next 7 sts; roll Shell so unworked front loops of a previous round line up with next stitches on current round; working on unworked front loops & current round, sc in each of next 4 sts; working on current round only, sc in next st. (12 sc) *(images 10 - 13)*

Round 13: Working in **back loops** only, sc in each st around. (12 sc)

Round 14: Sc in each st around. (12 sc)

Round 15: Working in **back loops** only, sc in each st around. (12 sc)

Round 16: Sc in each of next 7 sts; roll Shell so unworked front loops of a previous round line up with next stitches on current round; working on unworked front loops & current round, sc in each of next 4 sts; working on current round only, sc in next st. (12 sc)

Round 17: Working in **back loops** only, sc in each st around. (12 sc)

Round 18: Sc in each st around. (12 sc)

Round 19: Working in **back loops** only, sc in each st around. (12 sc)

Round 20: Sc in each of next 7 sts; roll Shell so unworked front loops of a previous round line up with next stitches on current round; working on unworked front loops & current round, sc in each of next 4 sts; working on current round only, sc in next st. (12 sc)

Round 21: Working in **back loops** only, sc in each st around. (12 sc)

Round 22: Sc in each st around. (12 sc)

Round 23: Working in **back loops** only, sc in each st around. (12 sc)

Round 24: Sc in each of next 7 sts; roll Shell so unworked front loops of a previous round line up with next stitches on current round; working on unworked front loops & current round, sc in each of next 4 sts; working on current round only, sc in next st. (12 sc)

Round 25: Working in **back loops** only, sc in each st around. (12 sc)

Round 26: Sc in each st around. (12 sc)

Round 27: Working in **back loops** only, sc in each st around. (12 sc)

Round 28: Sc in each of next 7 sts; roll Shell so unworked front loops of a previous round line up with next stitches on current round; working on unworked front loops & current round, sc in each of next 4 sts; working on current round only, sc in next st. (12 sc)

Round 29: Working in **back loops** only, sc in each st around. (12 sc)

Round 30: Sc in each st around. (12 sc)

Round 31: Working in **back loops** only, sc in each st around. (12 sc)

Round 32: Sc in each of next 7 sts; roll Shell so unworked front loops of a previous round line up with next stitches on current round; working on unworked front loops & current round, sc in each of next 4 sts; working on current round only, sc in next st. (12 sc)

Round 33: Working in **back loops** only, sc in each st around. (12 sc)

Round 34: Sc in each st around. (12 sc)

Round 35: Working in **back loops** only, sc in each st around. (12 sc)

Round 36: Sc in each of next 7 sts; roll Shell so unworked front loops of a previous round line up with next stitches on current round; working on unworked front loops & current round, sc in each of next 4 sts; working on current round only, sc in next st. (12 sc)

Round 37: Working in **back loops** only, sc in each st around. (12 sc)

Round 38: Sc in each st around. (12 sc)

Round 39: Working in **back loops** only, sc in each st around. (12 sc)

Round 40: Sc in each of next 7 sts; roll Shell so unworked front loops of a previous round line up with next stitches on current round; working on unworked front loops & current round, sc in each of next 4 sts; working on current round only, sc in next st. (12 sc)

Round 41: Working in **back loops** only, sc in each st around. (12 sc)

Round 42: Sc in each st around. (12 sc)

Round 43: Working in **back loops** only, sc in each st around. (12 sc)

Note: In the next round, you will close the end of the Shell and attach it to unworked front loops of a previous round at the same time.

Closing Row: Sc in next st; flatten end of Shell; working through both layers of end of Shell *(to close opening)*, sl st in next st; working through both layers of end of Shell & closest unworked front loops of a previous round together *(across three layers)*, sc in each of next 4 sts; working through both layers of end of Shell, sl st in next st. (2 sl st & 4 sc) *(image 14)*

Fasten off and weave in end. Alternatively, crochet over end when Shell attached to Body.

BODY & HEAD

Round 1: With MC-1, make a magic ring, 6 sc in ring. (6 sc)

Round 2: [Sc in next st, inc in next st] 3 times. (9 sc)

Round 3: Sc in each st around. (9 sc)

Round 4: [Sc in each of next 2 sts, inc in next st] 3 times. (12 sc)

Round 5: Sc in each st around. (12 sc)

Note: In the next round, you will attach the Shell to the Body using unworked front loops on the Shell. Orienting the Shell so the closing stitches point towards the Body,

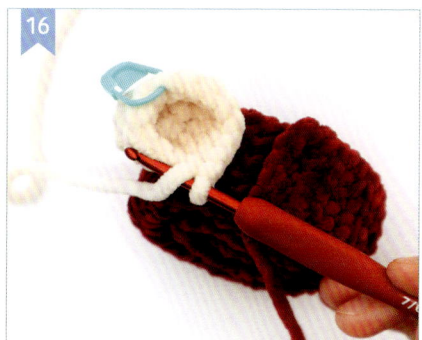

use the unworked front loops that are adjacent to the closing stitches (see photos). When attaching the Shell, hold the unworked front loops of the Shell against the next stitches on the Body. Work the "attaching" stitches through the Shell (in the unworked front loops) and the Body together, across both layers.

Round 6: Sc in each of next 4 sts; *(Attach Shell)* working on Shell *(in unworked front loops)* & Body, sc in each of next 4 sts; working on Body only, sc in each of next 4 sts. (12 sc) *(images 15 - 17)*

Rounds 7-8: *(2 rounds)* Sc in each st around. (12 sc)

*Note: In the next round, you will attach the Shell to the Body again but use the **front loops** only of the closing stitches of the Shell. When attaching the Shell, hold the closing stitches against the next stitches on the Body. Work the "attaching" stitches through the Shell (in **front loops** only) and the Body together, across both layers.*

Round 9: Sc in each of next 4 sts; *(Attach Shell)* working on Shell *(in **front loops** only)* & Body, sc in each of next 4 sts; working on Body only, sc in each of next 4 sts. (12 sc)

Rounds 10-11: *(2 rounds)* Sc in each st around. (12 sc)

Stuff lower part of Body lightly and continue to stuff as you go, increasing the amount of stuffing used in upper parts of Body.

Note: For Rounds 12, 15, 18 & 21, you will attach the Shell to the Body again. Use the same technique as Round 6 of Body, working into the next set of unworked front loops of Shell.

Round 12: Sc in each of next 4 sts; *(Attach Shell)* working on Shell *(in next set of unworked front loops)* & Body, sc in each of next 4 sts; working on Body only, sc in each of next 4 sts. (12 sc)

Rounds 13-14: *(2 rounds)* Sc in each st around. (12 sc)

Round 15: Sc in each of next 4 sts; *(Attach Shell)* working on Shell *(in next set of unworked front loops)* & Body, sc in each of next 4 sts; working on Body only, sc in each of next 4 sts. (12 sc)

Rounds 16-17: *(2 rounds)* Sc in each st around. (12 sc)

Round 18: Sc in each of next 4 sts; *(Attach Shell)* working on Shell *(in next set of unworked front loops)* & Body, sc in each of next 4 sts; working on Body only, sc in each of next 4 sts. (12 sc)

Rounds 19-20: *(2 rounds)* Sc in each st around. (12 sc)

Round 21: Sc in each of next 4 sts; *(Attach Shell)* working on Shell *(in next set of unworked front loops)* & Body, sc in each of next 4 sts; working on Body only, sc in each of next 4 sts. (12 sc) *(image 18)*

Round 22: Working in **front loops** only, inc in each st around. (24 sc)

Round 23: [Sc in each of next 2 sts, inc in next st] 8 times. (32 sc)

Rounds 24-26: *(3 rounds)* Sc in each st around. (32 sc)

Round 27: [Sc in each of next 2 sts, dec] 8 times. (24 sc)

Rounds 28-29: *(2 rounds)* Sc in each st around. (24 sc)

Insert safety eyes between Rounds 25 & 26, approximately 8 sts apart on either side of Head.

Stuff Head and continue to stuff as you go.

Round 30: [Sc in each of next 2 sts, dec] 6 times. (18 sc)

Round 31: [Sc in next st, dec] 6 times. (12 sc)

Orientation Check Point

In the next round, you want the puff stitches to sit on either side of the Head, in line with the Shell. If needed, move the start of round forward (by making additional single crochet stitches), or back (by removing single crochet stitches) to allow for this (the first puff stitch is the second stitch of the round). If you need to remove stitches that include a decrease, make sure you remake the decrease so you continue to have the correct stitch count.

Round 32: Sc in next st, puff in next st, sc in each of next 5 sts, puff in next st, sc in each of next 4 sts. (10 sc & 2 puff-sts)

Round 33: [Dec] 6 times. (6 sc)

Fasten off, leaving a long tail for sewing. Use yarn needle to weave yarn tail through front loops of final round and pull to close.

Face Details

1. With black embroidery floss, embrowider a straight line between the Eyes to make the Mouth and small diagonal Eyebrows 2 rounds above the Eyes.

3. Add blush for Cheeks (optional). *(image 19)*

SCARF

Row 1: With Color B, ch 41, sl st in 2nd ch from hook, sc in next ch, hdc in next ch, dc-inc in next ch, hdc in next ch, sc in each of next 30 ch, hdc in next ch, dc-inc in next ch, hdc in next ch, sc in next ch, sl st in next ch (2 sl sts, 32 sc, 4 hdc & 4 dc)

Fasten off and weave in end.

1. Tie the Scarf around the Snail's neck.

NASH THE HEDGEHOG

Do not worry about the prickles. Nash gives the softest hugs.

Skill Level: Advanced
Sewing Level: No-sew

Finished Size: 28 cm

Yarn:

Hobbii Honey Bunny (3.5 oz, 131 yds/100 g, 120 m)

Main Color (MC): Oatmilk (03) for Arms, Head, Body & Legs - 1 ball

Color A: Chocolate (12) for Nose, Body & Toes - 1 ball

Color B: Pink for Cheeks - small amount

Materials:

G-6 (4.00 mm) hook
Two 8 mm oval safety eyes
Stuffing
Stitch markers
Yarn needle
Scissors

Orientation Check Points

Read these instructions carefully prior to starting the next round. You may be asked to alter the position of the start of the round before continuing.

Special Stitches:

Loop Stitch (LoopSt):

Starting with a loop on your hook, insert hook in the next stitch. Using your index finger, pull your yarn downwards in front of your work to form a long loop. Yarn over and pull a loop through, ensuring you still have a long loop of yarn in front of your work. Yarn over and pull through both loops on hook.

Note: Loop Stitch Alternative - If you do not enjoy using the loop stitch then you can instead use a fluffy yarn and make standard single crochet stitches, decreases, and increases instead of the loops. Substitute out your Color A chenille yarn for 1 ball of Hobbii Peacock yarn instead.

Loop Stitch Decrease (LoopSt-dec):

Starting with a loop on your hook, insert hook into the front loop only of each of the next 2 stitches. Using your index finger, pull your yarn downwards in front of your work to form a long loop. Yarn over and pull a loop through both of the front loops, ensuring you still have a long loop of yarn in front of your work. Yarn over and pull through both loops on hook.

Loop Stitch Increase (LoopSt-inc):

Insert hook into the next stitch and complete the first Loop Stitch. Insert hook into the same stitch and complete the second Loop Stitch.

ARM (Make 2)

Round 1: With MC, make a magic ring, 6 sc in ring. (6 sc)

Round 2: Inc in each st around. (12 sc)

Rounds 3-4: *(2 rounds)* Sc in each st around. (12 sc)

Round 5: [Dec] 3 times, sc in each of next 6 sts. (9 sc)

Rounds 6-14: *(9 rounds)* Sc in each st around. (9 sc)

Sc in next st *(to move the end of round to side of Arm).*

Stuff lower 2/3 of Arm.

Closing Row: Flatten Arm; working through both layers *(to close opening)*, sc in each of next 4 sts. (4 sc)

Fasten off and weave in end. Alternatively, crochet over end when Arm attached to Body. *(image 1)*

HEAD

Round 1: With MC, make a magic ring, 6 sc in ring. (6 sc)

Round 2: Sc in each st around. (6 sc)

Round 3: Sc in each of next 2 sts, inc in each of next 2 sts, sc in each of next 2 sts. (8 sc)

Round 4: Sc in each of next 2 sts, inc in next st, sc in each of next 2 sts, inc in next st, sc in each of next 2 sts. (10 sc)

Round 5: Sc in each of next 3 sts, inc in next st, sc in each of next 2 sts, inc in next st, sc in each of next 3 sts. (12 sc)

Round 6: Sc in each of next 3 sts, inc in next st, sc in each of next 4 sts, inc in next st, sc in each of next 3 sts. (14 sc)

Round 7: Sc in each of next 5 sts, inc in next st, sc in each of next 2 sts, inc in next st, sc in each of next 5 sts. (16 sc) *(image 2)*

Round 8: Sc in each of next 4 sts, hdc-inc in each of next 8 sts, sc in each of next 4 sts. (8 sc & 16 hdc) PM on the 2 middle hdc-sts *(marks center of Head and will help with orientation).*

Round 9: Sc in each of next 4 sts, [sc in next st, inc in next st] 4 times, [inc in next st, sc in next st] 4 times, sc in each of next 4 sts. (32 sc)

Round 10: Sc in each of next 4 sts, [inc in next st, sc in each of next 2 sts] 4 times, [sc in each of next 2 sts, inc in next st] 4 times, sc in each of next 4 sts. (40 sc)

Rounds 11-13: *(3 rounds)* Sc in each st around. (40 sc)

> **Orientation Check Point**
>
> The next round should start centrally at the base of the Head (directly opposite the marked central hdc-sts in Round 8). If needed, move the start of round forward (by making additional single crochet stitches), or back (by removing single crochet stitches) to allow for this. To mark the center of each Ear for the next round, place markers on the **back loops** of the 11th and 30th stitches of Round 13 (see photo 3).

Note: A contrasting color has been used instead of Color A for some of the photos for clarity. The single crochet clusters in Round 14 will not be worked in again and are not included in overall stitch count. At the end of Round 14, you will make the opening for the Body. (image 3)

Round 14: Sc in each of next 10 sts, 6 sc in **front loop** of next st *(First Ear; this should be in front of marked back loop)*; change to Color A, LoopSt in each of next 18 sts; change to MC, 6 sc in **front loop** of next st *(Second Ear; this should be in front of marked back loop)*, sc in each of next 7 sts; change to Color A, ch 6, skip next 6 sts *(Body opening; **this will extend beyond end of round**).* *(images 4-6)*

Note: The next stitch you make will be the new start of round. Remove markers as you encounter them.

Round 15: LoopSt in each of next 7 sts, sc in next marked **back loop** *(behind First Ear)*, LoopSt in each of next 18 sts, sc in next marked **back loop** *(behind Second Ear)*, LoopSt in each of next 7 sts; working in ch-6, sc in each of next 6 ch. (32 LoopSt & 8 sc)

Do not fasten off.

Face Details

1. Insert safety eyes between Rounds 8 & 9 on either side of the face.

2. With Color B, embroider small cheeks on the lower outer aspects of the eyes. With black thread embroider small eyebrows 2 rounds above the eyes.

3. With Color A, embroider the nose through the magic ring of the Head and over Rounds 2-3, forming a triangular shape (shown in Color B in photos). *(image 7)*

Continue with Head. *(image 8)*

Rounds 16-18: *(3 rounds)* LoopSt in each st around. (40 sts)

Round 19: [LoopSt in each of next 3 sts, dec] 8 times. (32 sts)

Stuff Head.

Round 20: [LoopSt in each of next 2 sts, dec] 8 times. (24 sts)

Round 21: [LoopSt in next st, dec] 8 times. (16 sts)

Round 22: [LoopSt-dec] 8 times. (8 sts)

Fasten off, leaving a long tail for sewing. Use yarn needle to weave yarn tail through front loops of final round and pull to close. *(image 9)*

BODY

Note: In the next round, you will be working around the Body opening made in Round 14 of the Head, starting in the ch-6. The stitch markers in photos mark the corner spaces of Body opening. (image 10)

Round 1: Attach Color A at center back of Body opening *(3 ch-sts away from next corner space)*, sc in same ch, sc in each of next 2 ch; change to MC, inc in next corner

space between rounds, sc in each of next 6 sts, inc in next corner space between rounds; change to Color A, sc in each of next 3 ch. (16 sc)

Round 2: Sc in next st, inc in next st, sc in next st; change to MC, inc in next st, [sc in next st, inc in next st] 2 times, [inc in next st, sc in next st] 2 times, inc in next st; change to Color A, sc in next st, inc in next st, sc in next st. (24 sc)

Orientation Check Point
The next round should start centrally at the back of the Body. If needed, move the start of round forward (by making additional single crochet stitches), or back (by removing single crochet stitches) to allow for this. If you need to remove stitches that include an increase, make sure you remake the increase so you continue to have the correct stitch count.

Note: In the next round (first two stitches and last two stitches), you will anchor the Head to the Body. This will prevent the Head from leaning forwards too much. When anchoring the Head, hold the side of the Head against the next stitches on the Body. Work each "attaching" stitch through the two closest stitch holes on the Head (inside then outside) and into the next stitch on the Body together, across both layers.

Note: In the next round, you will also be attaching the Arms. When attaching each Arm, hold the closing stitches of the Arm against the next stitches on the Body with the Arm decreases facing outwards. Work the "attaching" stitches through the Arm and the Body together, across both layers.

Round 3: *(Attach Head)* working on Head & Body, sc in each of next 2 sts; working on Body only, sc in each of next 2 sts; change to MC; *(Attach First Arm)* working on First Arm & Body, sc in each of next 4 sts; working on Body only, sc in each of next 8 sts; *(Attach Second Arm)* working on Second Arm & Body, sc in each of next 4 sts; change to Color A; working on Body only, sc in each of next 2 sts; *(Attach Head)* working on Head & Body, sc in each of next 2 sts. (24 sts) *(images 11 - 14)*

Round 4: LoopSt in each of next 2 sts, LoopSt-inc in next st, LoopSt in next st; change to MC, sc in next st, inc in next st, [sc in each of next 2 sts, inc in next st] 2 times, [inc in next st, sc in each of next 2 sts] 2 times, inc in next st, sc in next st; change to Color A, LoopSt in next st, LoopSt-inc in next st, LoopSt in each of next 2 sts. (32 sts)

Rounds 5-6: *(2 rounds)* LoopSt in each of next 5 sts; change to MC, sc in each of next 22 sts; change to Color A, LoopSt in each of next 5 sts. (32 sts)

Orientation Check Point
The next round should start centrally at the back of the Body. If needed, move the start of round forward (by making additional stitches), or back (by removing stitches) to allow for this.

Round 7: LoopSt in each of next 3 sts, LoopSt-inc in next st, LoopSt in next st; change to MC, sc in each of next 2 sts, inc in next st, [sc in each of next 3 sts, inc in next st] 2 times, [inc in next st, sc in each of next 3 sts] 2 times, inc in next st, sc in each of next 2 sts; change to Color A, LoopSt in next st, LoopSt-inc in next st, LoopSt in each of next 3 sts. (40 sts)

Rounds 8-10: *(3 rounds)* LoopSt in each of next 6 sts; change to MC, sc in each of next 28 sts; change to Color A, LoopSt in each of next 6 sts. (40 sts)

Orientation Check Point
The next round should start centrally at the back of the Body. If needed, move the start of round forward (by making additional stitches), or back (by removing stitches) to allow for this.

Round 11: LoopSt in each of next 6 sts; change to MC, sc in each of next 6 sts, [sc in next st, inc in next st] 4 times, [inc in next st, sc in next st] 4 times, sc in each of next 6 sts; change to Color A, LoopSt in each of next 6 sts. (48 sts)

Rounds 12-14: *(3 rounds)* LoopSt in each of next 6 sts; change to MC, sc in each of next 36 sts; change to Color A, LoopSt in each of next 6 sts. (48 sts)

Orientation Check Point
The next round should start centrally at the back of the Body. If needed, move the start of round forward (by making additional stitches), or back (by removing stitches) to allow for this.

Rounds 15-16: *(2 rounds)* LoopSt in each of next 6 sts; change to MC, sc in each of next 36 sts, change to Color A, LoopSt in each of next 6 sts. (48 sts)

Round 17: LoopSt in each of next 6 sts; change to MC, sc in each remaining st round. (48 sts)

Cut Color A and secure end.

Orientation Check Point
The next round should start centrally at the back of the Body. If needed, move the start of round forward (by making additional single crochet stitches), or back (by removing single crochet stitches) to allow for this.

Round 18: Sc in each of next 12 sts, [dec, sc in next st] 8 times, sc in each of next 12 sts. (40 sc)

Round 19: [Sc in each of next 3 sts, dec] 8 times. (32 sc)

Round 20: [Sc in each of next 2 sts, dec] 8 times. (24 sc)

Stuff Body. *(images 15 - 17)*

Do not fasten off. Continue with Legs.

LEGS

Leg Openings: Join the two central stitches at front of Body to the two central stitches at back of Body with stitch markers *(see photo; the Leg openings on either side of the markers should have 10 sts each)*, sc until you reach first marked central st, [sl st through **front loop** of next central st and **front loop** of opposite central st together, across both layers] 2 times *(these sl sts will not be worked into again and are not included in overall stitch count)*.

Do not fasten off. Continue with First Leg.

First Leg

Note: Work into the 10 sts of the first Leg opening only. The next st will be the new start of round. (image 18)

Round 1: Sc in each of next 10 sts. (10 sc)

Round 2: Insert hook in same st as last st and then from inside to outside through the first st of the previous round and make a sc across both layers *(this will prevent gaps)*, sc in each of next 9 sts. (10 sc) *(image 19)*

Rounds 3-4: *(2 rounds)* Sc in each st around. (10 sc)

Round 5: Working in **front loops** only, inc in each st around. (20 sc)

Rounds 6-8: *(3 rounds)* Sc in each st around. (20 sc)

Stuff Leg firmly.

Round 9: [Dec] 10 times. (10 sc)

Round 10: [Dec] 5 times. (5 sc)

Fasten off, leaving a long tail for sewing. Use yarn needle to weave yarn tail through front loops of final round and pull to close.

Second Leg

Attach MC to the unworked stitch on second Leg opening next to the central joining slip stitch (see photo). *(image 20)*

Rounds 1-10: *(10 rounds)* Repeat Rounds 1-10 of First Leg.

Fasten off, leaving a long tail for sewing. Use yarn needle to weave yarn tail through front loops of final round and pull to close.

1. With Color A, embroider 2 vertical lines on each foot for the paws. *(image 21)*

KORA THE KOALA

After a large bowl of eucalyptus leaves, Kora the Koala likes nothing more than a long nap, followed by a snooze, followed by 40 winks.

Skill Level: Advanced
Sewing Level: No-sew

Finished Size: 22 cm

Yarn:

Hobbii Honey Bunny (3.5 oz, 131 yds/100 g, 120 m)

Main Color (MC): Baby Blue (75) for Legs, Arms, Head & Body - 1 ball

Color A: Black (124) for Head – 1 ball

Color B: Hint of Pink (50) for Legs – 1 ball

Hobbii Peacock (3.5 oz, 71 yds/100 g, 65 m)

Color C: White (01) for Ear Fluff - 1 ball

Color D: Light Blue (08) for Neck Fluff - 1 ball

Hobbii Toucan (3.5 oz, 131 yds/100 g, 120 m)

Color E: Cotton Candy (16) for cheeks – small amount

Materials:

G-6 (4.00 mm) hook

Two 8 mm oval safety eyes

Stuffing

Stitch markers or scraps of yarn to mark stitches (19 required)

Yarn needle

Scissors

Orientation Check Points

Read these instructions carefully prior to starting the next round. You may be asked to alter the position of the start of the round before continuing.

Special Stitches:

½ Puff Stitch (½-puff):

Starting with a loop on your hook, yarn over and insert hook in the next stitch. Yarn over and pull a loop through (3 loops on hook). Yarn over and pull through 2 loops on hook (2 loops remain on hook). Repeat this process into the **same stitch** 1 more time (3 loops remain on hook). Yarn over and pull through all loops on hook.

Puff Stitch (puff):

Starting with a loop on your hook, yarn over and insert hook in the next stitch. Yarn over and pull a loop through (3 loops on hook). Yarn over and pull through 2 loops on hook (2 loops remain on hook). Repeat this process into the **same stitch** 4 more times (6 loops remain on hook). Yarn over and pull through all loops on hook.

LEG (Make 2)

Round 1: With Color B, make a magic ring, 8 sc in ring. (8 sc)

Round 2: Inc in each st around. (16 sc) Change to MC.

Round 3: Sc in each of next 4 sts, inc in each of next 8 sts, sc in each of next 4 sts. (24 sc)

Round 4: Sc in each of next 8 sts, [½-puff in next st, sc in next st] 2 times, [sc in next st, ½-puff in next st] 2 times, sc in each of next 8 sts. (20 sc & 4 ½-puff-sts)

Round 5: Sc in each st around. (24 sc)

Round 6: Sc in each of next 4 sts, [sc in each of next 2 sts, dec] 4 times, sc in each of next 4 sts. (20 sc)

Round 7: Sc in each of next 4 sts, [sc in next st, dec] 4 times, sc in each of next 4 sts. (16 sc)

Rounds 8-9: (2 rounds) Sc in each st around. (16 sc) Stuff the Leg firmly.

Round 10: [Sc in each of next 2 sts, dec] 4 times. (12 sc)

Fasten off and weave in end. Alternatively, crochet over end when Leg is attached to Body. *(image 1)*

ARM (Make 2)

Round 1: With MC, ch 4; sc in 2nd ch from hook, sc in next ch, 3 sc in last ch; working on other side of starting ch, sc in next ch, inc in last ch. (8 sc)

Round 2: Inc in next st, sc in next st, inc in each of next 3 sts, sc in next st, inc in each of next 2 sts. (14 sc)

Round 3: [½-puff in next st, sc in next st] 3 times, sc in each of next 8 sts. (3 ½-puff-sts & 11 sc)

Round 4: [Dec] 3 times, sc in each of next 8 sts. (11 sc)

Rounds 5-9: *(5 rounds)* Sc in each st around. (11 sc) Stuff Arm.

Round 10: [Dec] 3 times, sc in each of next 5 sts. (8 sc)

Orientation Check Point

Flatten the top of the Arm so that all the ½-puff stitches are on one side (parallel to the flattened end). You want the end of round to be to one side of the flattened end. If needed, work additional single crochet stitches to move the end of round to the side of the Arm.

Closing Row: Flatten Arm, ch 1; working through both layers *(to close opening)*, sc in each of next 4 sts. (4 sc)

Fasten off and weave in end. Alternatively, crochet over end when Leg is attached to Body.

HEAD

Round 1: With Color A, ch 4; sc in 2nd ch from hook, sc in next ch, 3 sc in last ch; working on other side of starting ch, sc in next ch, inc in last ch. (8 sc)

Round 2: Inc in next st, sc in next st, inc in next st, 3 sc in next st, inc in next st, sc in next st, inc in next st, 3 sc in next st. (16 sc)

Round 3: Sc in each st around. (16 sc) Fasten off. *(image 2)*

Round 4: Attach MC to one of center peaks of oval (see photo), sc in each st around. (16 sc)

Round 5: Sc in each of next 4 sts, hdc-inc in each of next 8 sts; PM on 2 middle hdc-sts *(marks center of Head and will help with orientation)*; sc in each of next 4 sts. (8 sc & 16 hdc)

Round 6: Sc in each of next 4 sts, [sc in next st, inc in next st] 4 times, [inc in next st, sc in next st] 4 times, sc in each of next 4 sts. (32 sc)

Round 7: Sc in each of next 4 sts, [inc in next st, sc in each of next 2 sts] 4 times, [sc in each of next 2 sts, inc in next st] 4 times, sc in each of next 4 sts. (40 sc)

Rounds 8-10: *(3 rounds)* Sc in each st around. (40 sc)

Orientation Check Point

The next round should start centrally at the base of the Head (directly opposite the marked central hdc-sts in Round 5). If needed, move the start of round forward (by making additional single crochet stitches), or back (by removing single crochet stitches) to allow for this. To mark the center of each Ear for the next round, place markers on the **back loops** of the 11th and 30th stitches of Round 10 (see photo). *(image 3)*

Note: The ears are a bit tricky. Take your time. Mark stitches where instructed; they will help you identify stitches you will need to work into during the following round. The stitches that make up the Ears are not included in overall stitch count. At the end of Round 11, you will start to make the opening for the Body.

Round 11: Sc in each of next 9 sts; do not fasten off; continue to First Ear, working in rows.

First Ear

Row 1: Skip next st; PM on skipped st; *(image 4)* 8 dc in **front loop** of next st *(this should be in front of stitch marker indicating center of Ear)*, skip next st; PM on skipped st; sl st in **front loop** of next st; PM on unworked **back loop** of same st; ch 2, skip next st; PM on skipped st; sl st in **front loop** of next st; PM on unworked **back loop** of same st. *(image 5)*

Row 2: Turn; skipping to dc-sts from Row 1, hdc-inc in each of next 8 dc, *(image 6)* skip next st *(on Head)*; PM on skipped st; sl st in **back loop** of next st *(on Head)*; PM on unworked **front loop** of same st.

Row 3: Turn; skipping to hdc-sts from Row 2, sl st in each of next 16 hdc. Do not fasten off. Continue on Head. *(image 7)*

Round 11 continued: Working on Head, sc in each of next 13 sts; do not fasten off; continue to Second Ear, working in rows.

Second Ear

Rows 1-3: *(3 rows)* Repeat Rows 1-3 of First Ear. Do not fasten off. Continue on Head.

Round 11 continued: Working on Head, sc in each of next 3 sts, ch 6, skip last 3 sts.

*Note: At the start of the next round, you will complete the opening for the Body. You will also be working into the marked unworked loops (in **back loop** only) and skipped stitches (in both loops) behind each Ear. Fold the ears downwards onto the face as you work behind them.*

Round 12: Skip next 3 sts *(Body opening)*, sc in each of next 3 sts; move start of round marker to 4th ch of ch-6 from Round 11; sc through inner edge of First Ear and next st on Head together across both layers; working behind First Ear and removing markers as you encounter them, *(image 8)* sc in each of next 8 marked sts; working on Head, *(images 9 -12)* sc in each of next 10 sts; sc through first st on Second Ear and next st on Head together across both layers; working behind Second Ear and removing markers as you encounter them, sc in each of next 8 marked sts; working on Head, sc in each of next 3 sts; working in ch-6, sc in each of next 3 ch. (37 sc & 3 ch-sts)

Round 13: Working in ch-6, sc in each of next 3 ch; sc in each remaining st around. (40 sc)

Rounds 14-16: *(3 rounds)* Sc in each st around. (40 sc)

Do not fasten off. Remove hook and place marker in working loop to secure it. Continue to Face Details and then Ear Fluff.

Face Details

1. Insert safety eyes on either side of the Nose at Round 5.

2. With Color E, embroider small Cheeks on the outer lower aspects of the Eyes. *(image 13)*

Ear Fluff

Note: In the photos, the Ears have been roughly divided into thirds using stitch markers for clarity.

1. Attach Color C at lower edge (marked with a pink stitch marker in photo) of First (left) Ear. Working in each stitch along the edge of the First Ear, make hdc in the lower 1/3 of the ear, sc in the middle 1/3 and sl sts in the upper 1/3. Fasten off.

2. Attach Color C at top edge of Second (right) Ear. Working in each stitch along the edge of the Second Ear, make sl sts in the upper 1/3 of the ear, sc in the middle 1/3 and hdc in the lower 1/3. Fasten off. (Photo – Koala ear fluff 1)

3. Pull the yarn tails inside the Head with your hook and knot them together to secure.

Start to stuff Head and continue to stuff as you go. Insert hook in marked working loop of Head and continue.

Round 17: [Sc in each of next 3 sts, dec] 8 times. (32 sc)

Round 18: [Sc in each of next 2 sts, dec] 8 times. (24 sc)

Round 19: [Sc in next st, dec] 8 times. (16 sc)

Round 20: [Dec] 8 times. (8 sc)

Fasten off, leaving a long tail for sewing. Use yarn needle to weave yarn tail through front loops of final round and pull to close. *(images 14 - 17)*

BODY

Note: In the next round, you will be working around the Body opening made in Rounds 11 and 12 of the Head, starting in the ch-6. The stitch markers in the photo mark the corner spaces of Body opening. (images 18 & 19)

Round 1: Attach MC at center back of Body opening *(3 ch-sts away from next corner space)*, sc in same ch, sc in each of next 2 ch, inc in next corner space between rounds, sc in each of next 6 sts, inc in next corner space between rounds, sc in each of next 3 ch. (16 sc)

Round 2: Working in **back loops** only, [sc in next st, inc in next st] 8 times. (24 sc)

*Note: In the next round, you will attach the Arms. When attaching each Arm, hold the closing stitches of the Arm against the next stitches on the Body with the Arm ½-puff stitches facing outwards. Work the "attaching" stitches through the Arm (in both loops) and the Body (in **back loop** only) together, across both layers.*

Round 3: Working in **back loops** only, sc in each of next 4 sts; (Attach First Arm) working on First Arm (in both loops) & Body (in **back loop** only), sc in each of next 4 sts; working on Body only (in **back loops** only), sc in each of next 8 sts; (Attach Second Arm) working on Second Arm (in both loops) & Body (in **back loop** only), sc in each of next 4 sts; working on Body only (in **back loops** only), sc in each of next 4 sts. (24 sc) *(images 20 & 21)*

Round 4: [Sc in each of next 2 sts, inc in next st] 8 times. (32 sc)

Rounds 5-6: *(2 rounds)* Sc in each st around. (32 sc)

Round 7: [Sc in each of next 3 sts, inc in next st] 8 times. (40 sc)

Rounds 8-13: *(6 rounds)* Sc in each st around. (40 sc)

Orientation Check Point

The next round should start centrally at the back of the Body. If needed, move the start of round forward (by making additional single crochet stitches), or back (by removing single crochet stitches) to allow for this.

Note: In the next round, you will attach the Legs. The position of each Leg has been mapped out with pink and green stitch markers in the photo. When attaching each Leg, hold the 6 sts at the front of the Leg (you will only work into these front 6 sts; the remaining sts are left unworked this round) against the next stitches on the Body with the ½-puff stitches pointing towards the Body. Work the "attaching" stitches through the Leg (from inside to outside) and the Body together, across both layers. (image 22)

Round 14: Sc in each of next 10 sts; (Attach First Leg) working on First Leg *(in front 6 sts)* & Body, sc in each of next 6 sts; PMs on 1st and 6th attaching sts; working on Body only, sc in each of next 8 sts; (Attach Second Leg) working on Second Leg *(in front 6 sts)* & Body, sc in each of next 6 sts; PMs on 1st and 6th attaching sts; working on Body only, sc in each of next 10 sts. (40 sc) *(images 23 & 24)*

Note: In the next round, you will crochet into the unworked stitches of each Leg. The attaching stitches from the previous round are not worked into again and are not included in overall stitch count.

Round 15: Sc in each of next 9 sts, insert hook from inside to outside through next st on Body and then from outside to inside through same stitch in First Leg as first marked attaching stitch and sc across both layers; working on First Leg, sc in each of next 6 sts, insert hook from inside to outside through same stitch in First Leg as second marked attaching stitch and then from outside to inside through next st on Body and sc across both layers; working on Body, sc in each of next 6 sts, , insert hook from inside to outside through next st on Body and then from outside to inside through same stitch in Second Leg as first marked attaching stitch and sc across both layers; working on Second Leg, sc in each of next 6 sts, insert hook from inside to outside through same stitch in Second Leg as second marked attaching stitch and then from outside to inside through next st on Body and sc across both layers; working on Body, sc in each of next 9 sts. (40 sc) *(images 25 - 27)*

Stuff Body and Legs firmly and continue to stuff as you go. Remove stitch markers from the Legs.

Round 16: Puff in next st, sc in each of next 2 sts, dec, [sc in each of next 3 sts, dec] 7 times. (1 puff & 31 sc)

Round 17: [Sc in each of next 2 sts, dec] 8 times. (24 sc)

Round 18: [Sc in next st, dec] 8 times. (16 sc)

Round 19: [Dec] 8 times. (8 sc)

Fasten off, leaving a long tail for sewing. Use yarn needle to weave yarn tail through front loops of final round and pull to close. *(image 28)*

Neck Fluff

With the Head pointing down and the back facing you, attach Color D to first unworked front loop on Round 1 of Body.

Rounds 1-2: *(2 rounds)* Working in unworked front loops only, sc in each st around. *(image 29)*

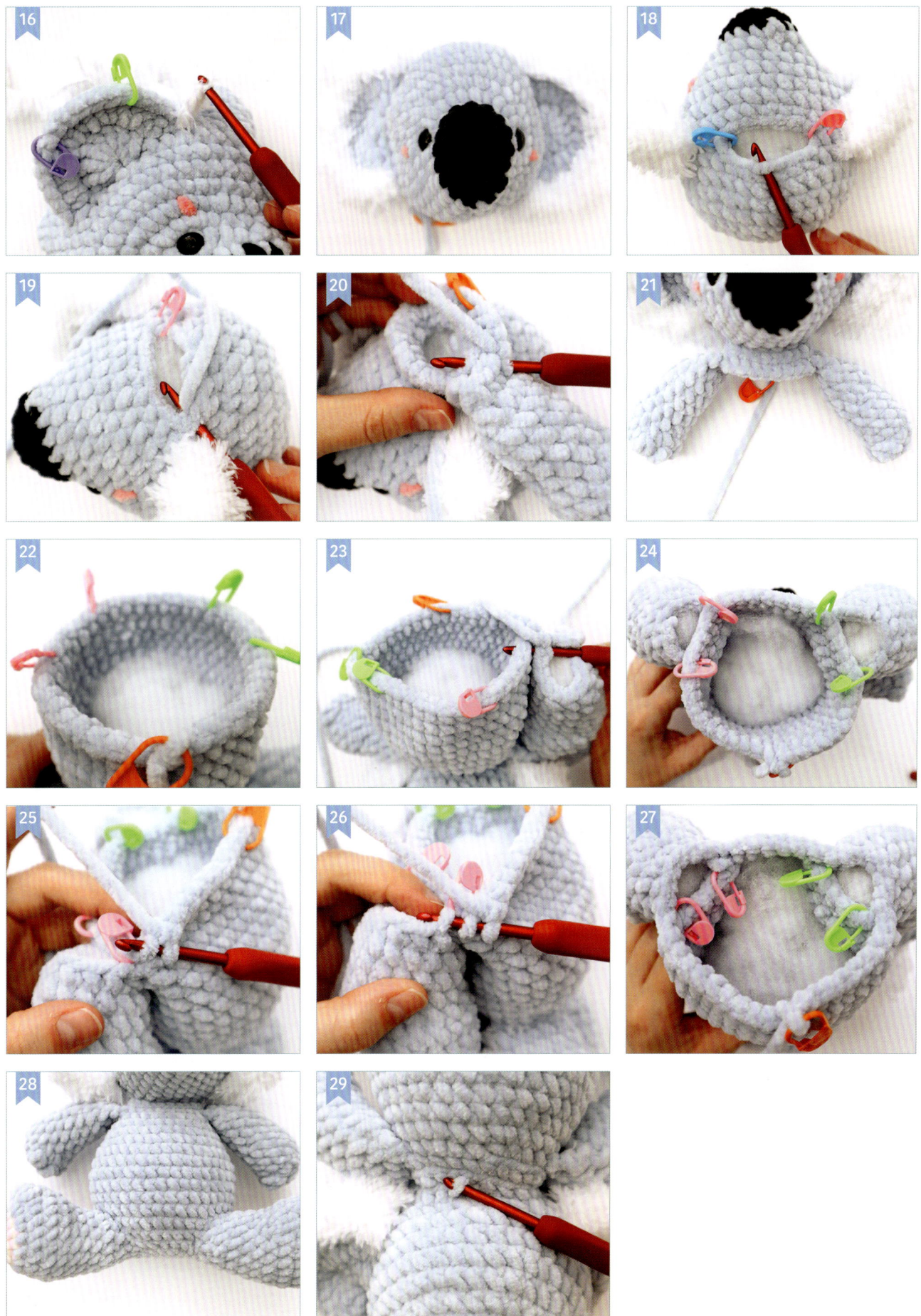

ZELDA THE LLAMA

Zelda loves a celebration. Her favorite food is birthday cake and her favorite color is rainbow. She is an expert at party games; however, she hates pinatas.

Skill Level: Intermediate
Sewing Level: No-sew

Finished Size: 20 cm

Yarn:

Hobbii Honey Bunny (3.5 oz, 131 yds/100 g, 120 m)

Main Color (MC): White (01) for Legs, Head, Body, Tail & Ears - 1 ball
Use Nougat (09) instead for the Brown Llama

Color A: Oatmilk (03) for Muzzle - 1 ball

Hobbii Toucan (3.5 oz, 131 yds/100 g, 120 m)

Color B: Oatmilk (03) for Legs - 1 ball
Use Cappuccino (30) instead for the Brown Llama

Color C: Cotton Candy (16) for Cheeks – small amount

Hobbii Toucan Fine (3.5 oz, 196 yds/100 g, 180 m) or light worsted cotton

Colors D, E & F: Accent colours of your choice for Harness & Blanket – small amounts

Materials:

G-6 (4.00 mm) hook (use unless told otherwise)

3.00 mm hook (for Bridle and Blanket)

Two 8 mm oval safety eyes

Stuffing

Stitch markers

Yarn needle

Scissors

Black embroidery floss

Orientation Check Points

Read these instructions carefully prior to starting the next round. You may be asked to alter the position of the start of the round before continuing.

MUZZLE

Round 1: With Color A, ch 4, inc in 2nd ch from hook, sc in next ch, 3 sc in last ch; working on other side of starting ch, sc in each of next 2 ch. (8 sc)

Round 2: [Sc in next st, inc in next st] 4 times. (12 sc)

Round 3: Sc in each st around. (12 sc)

Fasten off and weave in end. *(image 1)*

LEG (Make 4)

Round 1: With Color B, make a magic ring, 8 sc in ring. (8 sc)

Round 2: Sc in each st around. (8 sc)

Change to MC.

Round 3: [Sc in next st, inc in next st] 4 times. (12 sc)

Round 4: Sc in each st around. (12 sc)

Round 5: [Sc in each of next 2 sts, inc in next st] 4 times. (16 sc)

Round 6: Sc in each st around. (16 sc)

Fasten off and weave in end. Alternatively, crochet over ends when Legs are attached to Body. *(image 2)*

HEAD & BODY

Round 1: With MC, make a magic ring, 8 sc in ring. (8 sc)

Round 2: Inc in each st around. (16 sc)

Round 3: [Sc in next st, inc in next st] 8 times. (24 sc)

Rounds 4-6: *(3 rounds)* Sc in each st around. (24 sc)

Note: In the next round, you will attach the Muzzle. When attaching the Muzzle, hold 6 sts of the Muzzle (you will only work into these 6 sts; the remaining sts are left unworked this round) against the next stitches on the Head. Work the "attaching" stitches through the Muzzle (from inside to outside) and the Head together, across both layers.

Round 7: Sc in each of next 9 sts; *(Attach Muzzle)* working on Muzzle & Head, sc in each of next 6 sts; working on Head only, sc in each of next 9 sts. (24 sc) *(images 3 & 4)*

Note: In the next round, you will crochet into the unworked stitches of the Muzzle. The two stitches that are worked through the Head and Muzzle together help prevent gaps at the attachment points. The attaching stitches from the previous round are not worked into again and are not included in overall stitch count.

Round 8: Sc in each of next 8 sts, insert hook from inside to outside through next st on Head and then from outside to inside through same stitch in Muzzle as first attaching stitch and sc across both layers; working on Muzzle, sc in each of next 6 sts, insert hook from inside to outside through same stitch in Muzzle as last attaching stitch and then from outside to inside through next st on Head and sc across both layers; working on Head, sc in each of next 8 sts. (24 sc) *(images 5 - 8)*

Rounds 9-14: *(6 rounds)* Sc in each st around. (24 sc)

Do not fasten off.

Face Details

1. Insert safety eyes between Round 7 & 8 on either side of Muzzle.

2. With Color C, embroider Cheeks.

3. With black embroidery floss, embroider a T shaped Nose. Make 2 or 3 horizontal stitches, 4 stitches wide, centrally over Rounds 1-2 of the Muzzle, then make a vertical stitch down from the center.

4. Stuff Head. *(image 9)*

> **Orientation Check Point**
> The next round should start centrally at the back of the Head (opposite Muzzle). If needed, move the start of round forward by making additional single crochet stitches to allow for this.

Note: Starting in the next round, you will make the Body by working around a chain.

Round 15: Sc in next st, ch 7, sc in 2nd ch from hook, sc in each of next 5 ch; working on Head, sc in each of next 23 sts. (30 sc & 6 ch-sts) *(images 10 & 11)*

Round 16: Sc in next st; working in ch-7, sc in each of next 5 ch, inc in next ch; inc in next st, sc in each of next 28 sts. (38 sc)

Round 17: Sc in each of next 6 sts, inc in next st, sc in each of next 2 sts, inc in next st, sc in each of next 28 sts. (40 sc) *(image 12)*

Rounds 18-24: *(7 rounds)* Sc in each st around. (40 sc)

> **Orientation Check Point**
> Over the next two rounds, you will attach the Legs. Map out the position of each Leg before starting the round. Each Leg attaches to one corner of the Body over 8 sts with 2 sts between Legs. Start by identifying the center 2 stitches at the front of the Body (in line with the Muzzle; these will be between the front two Legs) and use stitch markers to mark the positions of the first and last (eighth) attaching stitches of each Leg, with 2 stitches between each Leg (see photo). The Legs may be joined in any order; however, you need to start the round at the start of one of the 2 stitch gaps between two Legs. If needed, move the start of round forward (by making additional single crochet stitches), or back (by removing single crochet stitches) to allow for this.

Note: When attaching each Leg, hold 8 sts of the Leg (you will only work into these 8 sts; the remaining sts are left unworked this round) against the next 8 stitches on the Body (indicated by your stitch markers). Work the "attaching" stitches through the Leg (from inside to outside) and the Body together, across both layers. (image 13)

Round 25: *Working on Body only, sc in each of next 2 sts; *(Attach Leg)* working on Leg & Body, sc in each of next 8 sts; remove markers indicating Leg position and place them on 1st and 8th attaching sts; repeat from * 3 more times. (40 sc) *(images 14 - 16)*

Note: In the next round, you will crochet into the unworked stitches of each Leg. The attaching stitches from the previous round are not worked into again and are not included in overall stitch count.

Round 26: Sc in next st, * insert hook from inside to outside through next st on Body and then from outside to inside through same stitch in Leg as first marked attaching stitch and sc across both layers; working on unworked sts of Leg, sc in each of next 8 sts, insert hook from inside to outside through same stitch in Leg as second marked attaching stitch and then from outside to inside through next st on Body and sc across both layers; repeat from * 3 more times **(this will extend beyond end of round by 1 st)**. (40 sc)

Stuff Body and Legs.

Round 27: [Sc in each of next 3 sts, dec] 8 times. (32 sc) Remove stitch markers on the Legs. *(image 17)*

Round 28: [Sc in each of next 2 sts, dec] 8 times. (24 sc)

Round 29: [Sc in next st, dec] 8 times. (16 sc)

Round 30: [Dec] 8 times. (8 sc)

Fasten off, leaving a long tail for sewing. Use yarn needle to weave yarn tail through front loops of final round and pull to close. *(image 18)*

TAIL

With MC, insert your hook inside then outside (through two stitch holes) between Rounds 16 & 17 at the back of the Body, just to the right of center, and pull a loop through.

Tail Loops: Ch 5, insert hook inside then outside through two stitch holes to the left and sl st, ch 7, insert hook inside then outside through two stitch holes to the left and sl st, ch 5, insert hook inside then outside through two stitch holes to the left and sl st. (3 loops)

Fasten off and hide ends inside Body. *(images 19 & 20)*

EARS

With MC, insert hook inside then outside (through two stitch holes) between Rounds 2 & 3 at the side of the Head and pull a loop through.

Ch 4, sl st in 2nd ch from hook, sc in next ch, hdc in next ch, insert hook inside then outside through two stitch holes on Head and sl st

Fasten off and hide ends inside Head. Repeat on opposite side of Head. *(images 21 - 24)*

HAIR

Note: The loops of Hair are made in a similar manner to the loops of the Tail. Make two rows of Hair at the front of the head between Rounds 2 & 3 and Rounds 3 & 4. (images 25 - 27)

With Color B, insert hook inside then outside (through two stitch holes) and pull a loop through.

Hair Loops: *Ch 5, insert hook inside then outside through two stitch holes and sl st; repeat from * until you have desired amount of Hair.

Fasten off and hide ends inside Head.

HARNESS

Use 3.00 mm hook and Color D, E, or F.

Leaving a yarn tail, make a ch that will fit around Muzzle and make note of the number of ch-sts *(number of ch-sts required = x)*, ch 25, sl st in xth ch from hook to form a ring *(example: if you needed 20 ch-sts to go around Muzzle, sl st into 20th ch)*, turn, working back around the ring, sl st in half the ch-sts in ring; ch 25.

Fasten off leaving a yarn tail. Put ring around Muzzle and tie yarn tails together. Trim ends.

BLANKET

With 3.00 mm hook and Colors D, E, and F, make each round of the Blanket a different color.

Round 1: Ch 21, sc in 2nd ch from hook, sc in each of next 18 ch, 3 sc in last ch; working on other side of starting ch, sc in each of next 18 ch, inc in last ch. (42 sc)

Round 2: Inc in next st, sc in each of next 18 sts, inc in each of next 3 sts, sc in each of next 18 sts, inc in each of next 2 sts. (48 sc)

Round 3: Dc-inc in each of next 4 sts, hdc in each of next 4 sts, sc in each of next 6 sts, hdc in each of next 4 sts, dc-inc in each of next 10 sts, hdc in each of next 4 sts, sc in each of next 6 sts, hdc in each of next 4 sts, dc-inc in each of next 6 sts. (40 dc, 16 hdc, 12 sc)

Fasten off and weave in ends.

ETHEL THE OSTRICH

Ethel is a fancy ostrich. She values good manners and politeness. Every day she ensures her feathers look perfect and places a beautiful bow around her neck.

Skill Level: Intermediate
Sewing Level: No-sew

Finished Size: 40 cm

Yarn:

Hobbii Honey Bunny (3.5 oz, 131 yds/100 g, 120 m)

Main Color (MC): White (01) for Head & Feathers - 1 ball

Color A: Silver (118) or Black (124) for Legs, Body & Tail - 1 ball (instructions are given to make a Silver Ostrich)

Color B: Hint of Pink (50) for Legs & Head - 1 ball

Hobbii Honey Bunny Candy (3.5 oz, 131 yds/100 g, 120 m)

Color C: Turquoise (94) for Bow & Collar-1 ball

Materials:

G-6 (4.00 mm) hook

Two 16 mm kawaii sinker safety eyes or Two 8mm oval safety eyes

Stuffing

Stitch markers

Yarn needle

Scissors

Black embroidery floss

Blush (optional)

Orientation Check Points
Read these instructions carefully prior to starting the next round. You may be asked to alter the position of the start of the round before continuing.

LEG (Make 2)

Round 1: With Color B, make a magic ring, 8 sc in ring. (8 sc)

Round 2: Sc in each of next 2 sts, inc in each of next 4 sts, sc in each of next 2 sts. (12 sc)

Round 3: Working in **back loops** only, sc in each st around. (12 sc)

Round 4: Sc in each of next 2 sts, [dec] 4 times, sc in each of next 2 sts. (8 sc)

Round 5: Sc in each of next 2 sts, [dec] 2 times, sc in each of next 2 sts. (6 sc)

Stuff foot and continue to stuff Leg as you go.

Rounds 6-12: *(7 rounds)* Sc in each st around. (6 sc)

Round 13: Sc in each st until you reach front of Leg, puff in next st, sc in each remaining st around. (5 sc & 1 puff)

Rounds 14-21: *(8 rounds)* Sc in each st around. (6 sc)

Change to Color A.

Round 22: Sc in each st around. (6 sc)

Sc in each st until you reach back of Leg *(to move the end of round)*.

Closing Row: Flatten Leg, ch 1; working through both layers *(to close opening)*, sc in each of next 3 sts. (3 sc)

Fasten off. *(image 1)*

HEAD

Round 1: With MC, make a magic ring, 8 sc in ring. (8 sc)

Round 2: Inc in each st around. (16 sc)

Round 3: [Sc in next st, inc in next st] 8 times. (24 sc)

Rounds 4-6: *(3 rounds)* Sc in each st around. (24 sc)

Note: In the next round you will start to make the beak by working around a chain.

Round 7: Sc in each of next 12 sts; change to Color B, ch 3; sc in 2nd ch from hook, sc in next ch; change to MC, sl st in same st as last MC sc made *(sl st will not be worked into again and is not included in overall st count)*, sc in each of next 12 sts. (26 sc & 2 ch-sts)

Round 8: Sc in each of next 11 sts; change to Color B, sc in next st; working in ch-3, sc in next ch, inc in next ch; inc in next st, sc in each of next 2 sts; change to MC, sc in each of next 11 sts. (30 sc)

Round 9: Sc in each of next 10 sts; change to Color B, sc in each of next 10 sts; change to MC, sc in each of next 10 sts. (30 sc)

Round 10: Sc in each of next 9 sts; change to Color B, sc in each of next 4 sts, [dec] 2 times, sc in each of next 4 sts; change to MC, sc in each of next 9 sts. (28 sc)

Round 11: Sc in each of next 10 sts; change to Color B, sc in each of next 2 sts, [dec] 2 times, sc in each of next 2 sts; change to MC, sc in each of next 10 sts. (26 sc)

Round 12: Sc in each of next 11 sts; change to Color B, [dec] 2 times; change to MC, sc in each of next 11 sts. (24 sc)

Cut Color B and secure end.

Do not fasten off.

Face Details

1. Insert safety eyes between Rounds 8 & 9 on either side of the Beak.
2. With black embroidery floss, embroider Eyelashes with a diagonal line at the top of the Eyes.
3. Add blush for Cheeks.

Continue with Head.

Rounds 13-18: *(6 rounds)* Sc in each st around. (24 sc)

Orientation Check Point
The next round should start centrally at the back of the Head (opposite Beak). If needed, move the start of round forward by making additional single crochet stitches to allow for this. *(images 2 & 3)*

Stuff Head. Do not fasten off. Continue to Body.

BODY

Note: Starting in the next round, you will form the Body by working around a chain.

Change to Color A.

Round 19: Sc in next st, ch 7; sc in 2nd ch from hook, sc in each of next 5 ch, sl st in same st as first sc of round *(sl st will not be worked into again and is not included in overall st count)*, sc in each of next 23 sts. (30 sc & 6 ch-sts)

Cut MC and secure end.

Round 20: Sc in next st; working in ch-7, sc in each of next 5 ch, inc in next ch; inc in next st, sc in each of next 28 sts. (38 sc)

Round 21: Sc in each of next 6 sts, [sc in next st, inc in next st] 2 times, sc in each of next 28 sts. (40 sc)

Round 22: Sc in each st around. (40 sc)

Orientation Check Point
In the next round we will make the Wings. This can be a little tricky. Take your time. I suggest using stitch markers to mark the position of each Wing before you start. The Wings sit on either side of the Body and Row 1 of each Wing is made over 4 stitches. There should be 20 stitches between the Wings at the back of the Body and 12 stitches between the Wings at the front of the Body. Find the center front of the Body and mark the front loops of the 7th and 10th stitches on either side of this center front point to mark the start and end of each Wing (4 markers total; see photo). The start of round should be at the marked 10th stitch on the Ostrich's left side. If needed, move the start of round forward (by making additional single crochet stitches), or back (by removing single crochet stitches) to allow for this. *(image 4)*

Round 23: Continue to First Wing, working in rows.

First Wing

Row 1: Ch 1, turn; working in **back loops** only, sc in each of next 4 sts. (4 sc)

Row 2: Ch 1, turn, inc in each of next 4 sts. (8 sc)

Row 3: Ch 1, turn, [sc in next st, inc in next st] 4 times. (12 sc)

Row 4: Ch 1, turn, [sc in each of next 2 sts, inc in next st] 4 times. (16 sc)

Row 5: Ch 1, turn, sc in each st across. (16 sc)

Row 6: Turn; working in **front loops** only, ch 7, sl st in first st *(same st ch-7 is worked from)*, (sl st, ch 7, sl st) in each of next 15 sts. (16 loops) *(images 5 - 15)*

Side of Wing: Working in sides of rows, sl st down side of First Wing to return to Round 23 of Body *(keep sl sts loose)*. Do not fasten off. Continue on Body.

Note: The stitches that make up the First Wing will not be worked into again and are not included in overall stitch count.

Round 23 continued: Working on Body, sc in each of next 24 sts; do not fasten off; continue with Second Wing, working in rows.

Second Wing

Rows 1-6: *(6 rows)* Repeat Rows 1-6 of First Wing.

Side of Wing: Working in sides of rows, sl st down side of Second Wing to return to Round 23 of Body *(keep sl sts loose)*. Do not fasten off. Continue on Body.

Note: *The stitches that make up the Second Wing will not be worked into again and are not included in overall stitch count.*

Round 23 continued: Working on Body, sc in each of next 12 sts, sc in each of next 4 unworked **back loops** behind First Wing. (40 sc) *(image 16)*

Note: *The next stitch made will be the new start of round.*

Round 24: Sc in each of next 20 sts, sc in each of next 4 unworked **back loops** behind Second Wing, sc in each of next 16 sts. (40 sc)

Rounds 25-27: *(3 rounds)* Sc in each st around. (40 sc)

Round 28: Sc in each of next 4 sts, [sc in each of next 2 sts, dec] 3 times, sc in each of next 8 sts, [sc in each of next 2 sts, dec] 3 times, sc in each of next 4 sts. (34 sc)

Start to stuff Body and continue to stuff as you go.

Round 29: Sc in each st around. (34 sc)

Round 30: Sc in each of next 4 sts, [sc in next st, dec] 3 times, sc in each of next 8 sts, [sc in next st, dec] 3 times, sc in each of next 4 sts. (28 sc)

Round 31: Sc in each of next 3 sts, [dec] 4 times, sc in each of next 6 sts, [dec] 4 times, sc in next st; leave remaining sts unworked. (18 sc & 2 unworked sts)

Note: *The next stitch made will be the new start of round.*

> **Orientation Check Point**
>
> In the next round, you will be attaching the Legs. The Legs should line up approximately with the Wings. The First Leg is attached at the start of the next Round. If needed, move the start of round forward (by making additional single crochet stitches), or back (by removing single crochet stitches) to allow for this. If you need to remove stitches that include a decrease, make sure you remake the decrease so you continue to have the correct stitch count.

Note: *When attaching each Leg, hold the closing stitches of the Leg against the next stitches on the Body with the Leg puff stitch facing the same direction as the beak. Work the "attaching" stitches through the Leg and the Body together, across both layers.*

Round 32: *(Attach First Leg)* working on First Leg & Body, sc in each of next 3 sts; working on Body only, sc in next st, dec, sc in each of next 2 sts, dec, sc in next st; *(Attach Second Leg)* working on Second Leg & Body, sc in each of next 3 sts; working on Body only, dec, sc in each of next 2 sts, dec. (16 sc) *(images 17 - 19)*

Round 33: [Dec] 8 times. (8 sc)

Fasten off, leaving a long tail for sewing. Use yarn needle to weave yarn tail through front loops of final round and pull to close.

TAIL

With Color A, insert your hook inside then outside (through two stitch holes) at the back of the Body, just to the right of center, and pull a loop through.

Tail Loops: Ch 5, insert hook inside then outside through two stitch holes to the left and sl st, ch 7, insert hook inside then outside through two stitch holes to the left and sl st, ch 5, insert hook inside then outside through two stitch holes to the left and sl st. (3 loops)

Fasten off. Use yarn needle to hide ends inside the Body. *(images 20 - 22)*

FEATHERS

Attach MC to first unworked **back loop** of Row 5 of First Wing.

Feather Loops: Working in unworked **back loops** only, ch 7, sl st in first st (same st ch-7 is worked from), (sl st, ch 7, sl st) in each of next 15 sts. (16 loops)

Repeat for Second Wing. *(images 23 & 24)*

BOW

Row 1: With Color C, ch 22; hdc in 3rd ch from hook, hdc in each of next 19 ch. (20 hdc)

Rows 2-5: *(4 rows)* Ch 2, turn; working in **back loops** only, hdc in each st across. (20 hdc)

Bow Edging: Do not turn; inc in corner; working in sides of rows, sc in each row until next corner; inc in corner; working on other side of starting chain, sc in each ch until next corner; inc in corner; working in sides of rows, sc in each row until next corner; inc in corner; working on Row 5, sl st in each st until middle of Row; ch 5, wrap chain around center of Bow, sl st in 1st ch *(forming a loop)*.

Fasten off and weave in end. *(images 25 - 29)*

COLLAR

Row 1: With Color C, leaving a long tail, ch 30; sc in 3rd ch from hook, sc in each of next 27 ch. (28 sc)

Fasten off, leaving a long tail.

ASSEMBLY

1. Wrap the Collar around Ostrich's neck.

2. Use your hook to pull one of the Collar's long tails through the back of the Bow and then through the other end of the Collar.

3. Tie the Collar's yarn tails together to secure.

ISLA THE OTTER

Ahoy! Cadet Isla loves to swim and sail. She is learning how to navigate by the stars and is planning for an epic voyage around the world with her otter friends.

Skill Level: Intermediate
Sewing Level: No-sew

Finished Size: 32 cm

Yarn:

Hobbii Honey Bunny (3.5 oz, 131 yds / 100 g, 120 m)

Hobbii Toucan (3.5 oz, 131 yds / 100 g, 120 m)

Main Color (MC): Toucan in Cappuccino (30) for Ears, Arms, Legs, Nose, Body & Tail - 1 ball

Color A: Honey Bunny in Oatmilk (03) for Head - 1 ball

Color B: Honey Bunny in White (01) for Head - 1 ball

Color C: Toucan in Cotton Candy for Cheeks – small amount (optional)

Color D: Toucan in Sky Blue (21) for Collar & Toggle - small amount

Materials:

G-6 (4.00 mm) hook

Two 8 mm oval safety eyes

Stuffing

Stitch markers

Yarn needle

Scissors

Black embroidery floss

Orientation Check Points

Read these instructions carefully prior to starting the next round. You may be asked to alter the position of the start of the round before continuing.

ARM (Make 2)

Round 1: With MC, make a magic ring, 8 sc in ring. (8 sc)

Round 2: Inc in each st around. (16 sc)

Rounds 3-4: *(2 rounds)* Sc in each st around. (16 sc)

Round 5: Sc in each of next 4 sts, [dec] 4 times, sc in each of next 4 sts. (12 sc)

Round 6: Sc in each of next 2 sts, [dec] 4 times, sc in each of next 2 sts. (8 sc)

Stuff Arm and continue to stuff lower 2/3 only.

Rounds 7-9: *(3 rounds)* Sc in each st around. (8 sc)

Closing Row: Flatten Arm, ch 1; working through both layers *(to close opening)*, sc in each of next 4 sts. (4 sc) Fasten off. *(image 1)*

LEG (Make 2)

Round 1: With MC, make a magic ring, 8 sc in ring. (8 sc)

Round 2: Inc in each st around. (16 sc)

Round 3: Sc in each of next 6 sts, inc in each of next 4 sts, sc in each of next 6 sts. (20 sc)

Rounds 4-6: *(3 rounds)* Sc in each st around. (20 sc)

Stuff foot of Leg.

Round 7: Sc in each of next 4 sts, [dec] 6 times, sc in each of next 4 sts. (14 sc)

Round 8: Sc in each of next 3 sts, [dec] 4 times, sc in each of next 3 sts. (10 sc)

Rounds 9-11: *(3 rounds)* Sc in each st around. (10 sc)

Stuff lower half of Leg.

Closing Row: Flatten Leg, ch 1; working through both layers *(to close opening)*, sc in each of next 5 sts. (5 sc) *(image 2)*

HEAD

Note: Contrasting colors are used in the photos for clarity.

Round 1: With Color B, ch 7; inc in 2nd ch from hook, sc in each of next 4 ch, 4 sc in last ch; working on other side of starting ch, sc in each of next 4 ch, inc in last ch. (16 sc)

Round 2: Inc in each of next 2 sts, sc in each of next 4 sts, inc in each of next 4 sts, sc in each of next 4 sts, inc in each of next 2 sts. (24 sc)

Round 3: [Sc in next st, inc in next st] 2 times, sc in each of next 4 sts, [inc in next st, sc in next st] 2 times, [sc in next st, inc in next st] 2 times, sc in each of next 4 sts, [inc in next st, sc in next st] 2 times. (32 sc)

Orientation Check Point
Mark the 2 central stitches on each long side of the oval with stitch markers (4 markers total). There should be 14 stitches between the pairs of markers on either side. *(image 3)*

Round 4: Sc in each st until first marked st; *(Join Marked Sts)* folding the oval in half long ways so opposite marked stitches match up, [sc in both loops of next marked st and **back loop** only of opposite marked st across both layers] 2 times; sc in each of next 14 sts, sc in each of next 2 unworked **front loops**; PM on st just made, sc in each remaining st around. (32 sc) *(images 4-7)*

Note: Head will now look bow shaped.

Fasten off and weave in end.

Note: Blue yarn has been used in the following photos instead of Color A to provide contrast. (image 8)

Round 5: Attach Color A to marked st from previous round, sc in same st, sc in each of next 7 sts, [hdc in next st, hdc-inc in next st] 4 times, [hdc-inc in next st, hdc in next st] 4 times, sc in each of next 8 sts. (16 sc & 24 hdc)

Note: In the next round, you will shape the face further. Pinch the Head so that the next 5 sts are against the last 5 sts of Round 5, with right sides facing each other. Use a stitch marker to help hold the folded shape temporarily. The joining stitches in the next round will not be worked in again and are not included in overall stitch count. (images 9 & 10)

Round 6: Ch 1; *(Join Folded Stitches)* matching the next 5 sts with the last 5 sts of Round 5 *(right sides facing)*, [sl st in next matching pair of sts together across both layers] 5 times, sc in each of next 6 sts, [sc in each of next 2 sts, inc in next st] 3 times, [inc in next st, sc in each of next 2 sts] 3 times, sc in each of next 6 sts. (36 sc) *(images 11 - 14)*

Round 7: Sc in each of next 6 sts, [inc in next st, sc in each of next 3 sts] 3 times, [sc in each of next 3 sts, inc in next st] 3 times, sc in each of next 6 sts. (42 sc) *(images 15 & 16)*

Rounds 8-10: *(3 rounds)* Sc in each st around. (42 sc)

Orientation Check Point
The next round should start centrally at the base of the Head. If needed, move the start of round forward (by making additional single crochet stitches), or back (by removing single crochet stitches) to allow for this.

Note: In the next round, you will make the Ears and start to make the opening for the Body. The Ears are positioned on the top of the Head, 12 stitches apart. To mark the position of each Ear, place markers on the back loops of the 15th and 28th stitches of Round 10 (see photo). The stitches that make up the Ears in Round 11 will not be worked in again and are not included in overall stitch count.

Round 11: Sc in each of next 14 sts; change to MC, (sc, hdc, 3 dc, ch 2, sl st) in **front loop** of next st *(First Ear)*; change to Color A, sc in each of next 12 sts; change to MC, (sl st, ch 2, 3 dc, hdc, sc) in **front loop** of next st *(Second Ear)*; change to Color A, sc in each of next 11 sts, ch 6, skip last 3 sts.

Round 12: Skip next 3 sts *(Body opening)*, sc in next st; move start of round marker to 4th ch of ch-6 from Round 11; sc in each of next 10 sts; removing markers as you encounter them, sc in **back loop** behind First Ear, sc in each of next 12 sts, sc in **back loop** behind Second Ear, sc in each of next 11 sts; working in ch-6, sc in each of next 3 ch. (39 sc & 3 ch-sts) *(images 17 - 19)*

Round 13: Working in ch-6, sc in each of next 3 ch; sc in each remaining st around. (42 sc)

Round 14: Sc in each st around. (42 sc) Do not fasten off.

Face Details

1. Insert safety eyes over Round 5 with a gap of 8 sts between them.

2. With MC, embroider the nose through the center of Round 1 of the Head and up and over Round 3, forming a triangular shape. Finish with one long horizontal stitch across the top of the nose. *(images 20 -22)*

3. With Color C, embroider small cheeks on the lower outer aspects of the safety eyes.

With black embroidery floss, embroider whiskers on either side of the face. Continue with Head.

Round 15: [Sc in each of next 5 sts, dec] 6 times. (36 sc)

Round 16: [Sc in each of next 4 sts, dec] 6 times. (30 sc)

Stuff Head.

Round 17: [Sc in each of next 3 sts, dec] 6 times. (24 sc)

Round 18: [Sc in next st, dec] 8 times. (16 sc)

Round 19: [Dec] 8 times. (8 sc)

Fasten off, leaving a long tail for sewing. Use yarn needle to weave yarn tail through front loops of final round and pull to close.

BODY

Note: In the next round, you will be working around the Body opening made in Rounds 12 and 13 of the Head, starting in the ch-6. The stitch markers in the photo mark the corner spaces of Body opening. (image 23)

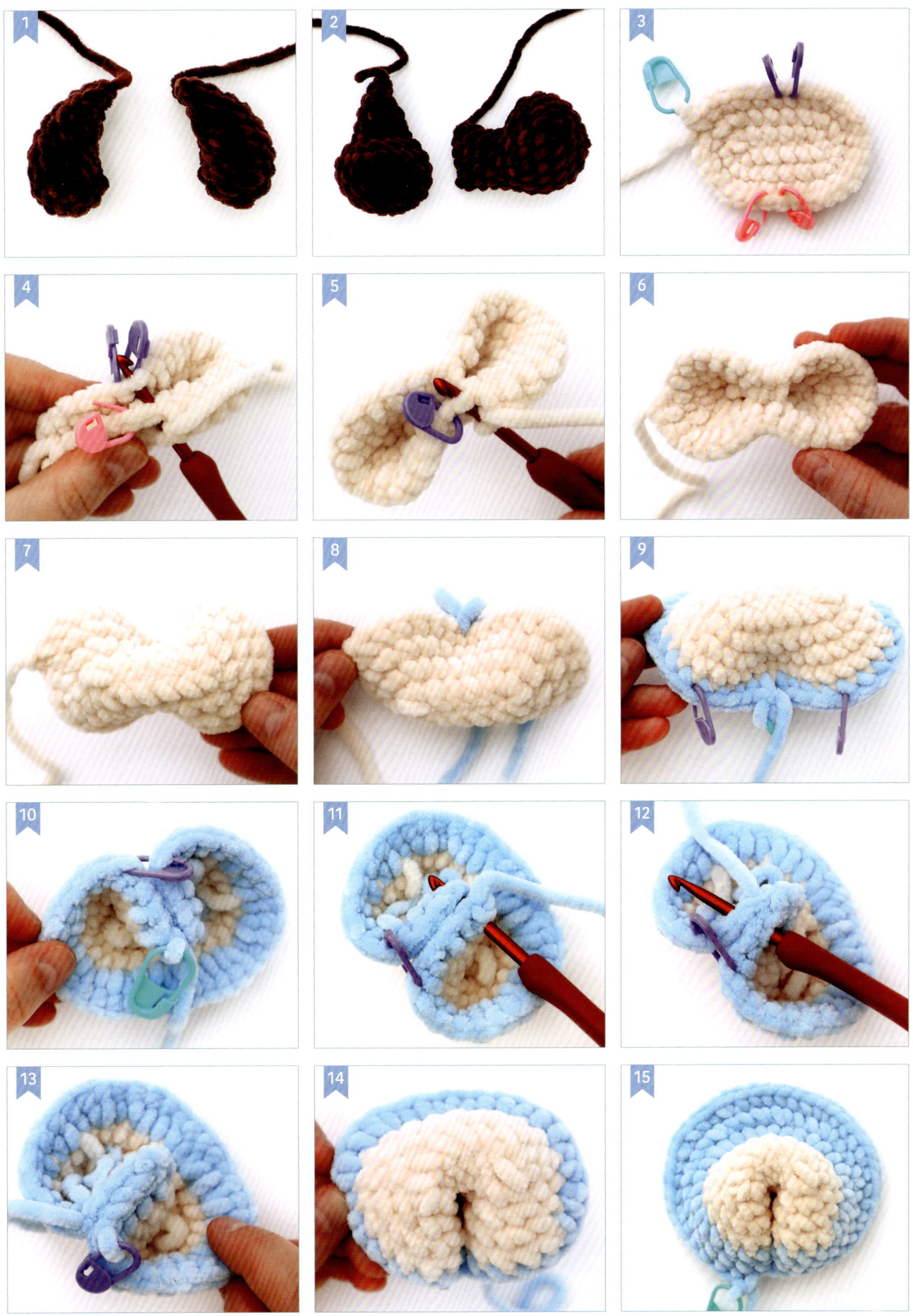

Round 1: Attach MC to center back of Body opening on Head *(3 ch-sts away from next corner space)*, sc in same ch, sc in each of next 2 ch, inc in next corner space between rounds, sc in each of next 6 sts, inc in next corner space between rounds, sc in each of next 3 ch. (16 sc)

Round 2: [Sc in next st, inc in next st] 8 times. (24 sc)

Orientation Check Point
The next round should start centrally at the back of the Body. If needed, move the start of round forward (by making additional single crochet stitches), or back (by removing single crochet stitches) to allow for this. If you need to remove stitches that include an increase, make sure you remake the increase so you continue to have the correct stitch count.

Note: In the next round, you will attach the Arms. When attaching each Arm, hold the closing stitches of the Arm against the next stitches on the Body with the decreases of the Arm facing outwards. Work the "attaching" stitches through the Arm and the Body together, across both layers.

Round 3: Sc in each of next 4 sts; *(Attach First Arm)* working on First Arm & Body, sc in each of next 4 sts; working on Body only, sc in each of next 8 sts; *(Attach Second Arm)* working on Second Arm & Body, sc in each of next 4 sts; working on Body only, sc in each of next 4 sts. (24 sc) *(images 24 & 25)*

Round 4: [Sc in each of next 2 sts, inc in next st] 8 times. (32 sc)

Rounds 5-6: *(2 rounds)* Sc in each st around. (32 sc)

Round 7: [Sc in each of next 3 sts, inc in next st] 8 times. (40 sc)

Rounds 8-9: *(2 rounds)* Sc in each st around. (40 sc)

Orientation Check Point
The next round should start centrally at the back of the Body. If needed, move the start of round forward (by making additional single crochet stitches), or back (by removing single crochet stitches) to allow for this.

Note: In the next round, you will attach the Legs. When attaching each Leg, hold the closing stitches of the Leg against the next stitches on the Body so that the foot points towards the front of the Bear once attached. Work each "attaching" stitch through the Leg and the Body together, across both layers.

Round 10: Sc in each of next 8 sts; *(Attach First Leg)* working on First Leg & Body, sc in each of next 5 sts; working on Body only, sc in each of next 14 sts; *(Attach Second Leg)* working on Second Leg & Body, sc in each of next 5 sts; working on Body only, sc in each of next 5 sts, inc in each of next 3 sts. (43 sc) *(images 26 & 27)*

Stuff Body.

Note: In the next round, you will start to make the opening for the Tail.

Round 11: Inc in each of next 3 sts, sc in each of next 34 sts, ch 6, skip next 6 sts. (40 sc & 6 ch-sts)

Round 12: Skip next 6 sts *(Tail opening)*, sc in next st; move start of round to sc just made; sc in each of next 2 sts, dec, [sc in each of next 3 sts, dec] 7 times *(working in ch-6 for last 6 sts)*. (32 sc) *(image 28)*

Round 13: [Sc in each of next 2 sts, dec] 8 times. (24 sc)

Round 14: [Sc in next st, dec] 8 times. (16 sc)

Round 15: [Dec] 8 times. (8 sc)

Fasten off, leaving a long tail for sewing. Use yarn needle to weave yarn tail through front loops of final round and pull to close.

TAIL

Note: In the next round, you will be working around the Tail opening made in Rounds 11 and 12 of the Body, starting in the ch-6. The stitch markers in the photo mark the corner spaces of the Tail opening. (image 29)

Round 1: With Head pointing down and facing you, attach MC to first ch-st on right side of ch-6 from Round 11, sc in same ch, sc in each of next 5 ch, sc in next corner space between rounds, sc in each of next 12 sts, sc in next corner space between rounds. (20 sc)

Round 2: Sc in each st around. (20 sc)

Round 3: Sc in each of next 7 sts, dec, sc in each of next 8 sts, dec, sc in next st. (18 sc)

Rounds 4-5: *(2 rounds)* Sc in each st around. (18 sc)

Round 6: [Sc in each of next 7 sts, dec] 2 times. (16 sc)

Rounds 7-8: *(2 rounds)* Sc in each st around. (16 sc)

Round 9: [Sc in each of next 6 sts, dec] 2 times. (14 sc)

Rounds 10-12: *(3 rounds)* Sc in each st around. (14 sc)

Round 13: [Sc in each of next 5 sts, dec] 2 times. (12 sc)

Rounds 14-16: *(3 rounds)* Sc in each st around. (12 sc)

Round 17: [Dec, sc in each of next 4 sts] 2 times. (10 sc)

Rounds 18-20: *(3 rounds)* Sc in each st around. (10 sc)

Round 21: [Dec, sc in each of next 3 sts] 2 times. (8 sc)

Rounds 22-24: *(3 rounds)* Sc in each st around. (8 sc)

Do not stuff. Fasten off, leaving a long tail for sewing. Use yarn needle to weave yarn tail through front loops of final round and pull to close.

COLLAR

Row 1: With Color D, ch 41; sl st in 2nd ch from hook, sc in next ch, hdc in next ch, dc-inc in next ch, hdc in next ch, sc in each of next 30 ch, hdc in next ch, dc-inc in next ch, hdc in next ch, sc in next ch, sl st in next ch. (42 sts)

Fasten off and weave in ends.

TOGGLE

Round 1: With Color D, ch 7; taking care not to twist ch, join with sl st in first ch to form a ring; ch 1, sc in each ch around. (7 sc)

Fasten off and weave in ends.

1. Wrap the collar around the Otter's neck and slide both ends through the Toggle.

SAMMIE THE PANDA & BABY LOU

Being a new mother isn't always easy, but Sammie is trying her best. She misses her sleep, but baby Lou's smile makes everything worthwhile.

Skill Level: Intermediate
Sewing Level: No-sew

Finished Size:
Sammie 22 cm & Baby Lou 15 cm

Yarn:

Hobbii Honey Bunny (3.5 oz, 131 yds/100 g, 120 m)

Main Color (MC): White (01) for Legs, Head & Body of Mamma and Head & Body of Baby - 1 ball

Color A: Silver (118) or Black (124) for Ears, Tail, Arms, Head & Body of Mamma and Head & Body for Baby - 1 ball

Color B: Black (124) for Nose of Mamma – small amount

Hobbii Toucan (3.5 oz, 131 yds/100 g, 120 m)

Color C: Cotton Candy (16) for Legs & Cheeks of Mamma and Nose & Cheeks of Baby – ¼ ball

Materials:

G-6 (4.00 mm) hook

Two 18 mm kawaii sinker eyes for Mamma & two 20 mm kawaii sinker eyes for Baby (alternatively, use black safety eyes with circles of colored felt behind)

Stuffing

Stitch markers

Yarn needle

Scissors

Black embroidery floss

Orientation Check Points

Read these instructions carefully prior to starting the next round. You may be asked to alter the position of the start of the round before continuing.

Special Stitches:

Puff Stitch (puff):

Starting with a loop on your hook, yarn over and insert hook in the next stitch. Yarn over and pull a loop through (3 loops on hook). Yarn over and pull through 2 loops on hook (2 loops remain on hook). Repeat this process into the **same stitch** 4 more times (6 loops remain on hook). Yarn over and pull through all loops on hook.

MAMMA PANDA

EAR (Make 2)

Round 1: With Color A, make a magic ring, 6 sc in ring. (6 sc)

Round 2: Inc in each st around. (12 sc)

Round 3: [Dec] 6 times. (6 sc)

Stuff Ear lightly.

Fasten off and weave in end. Alternatively, crochet over end when Ear attached to Head.

TAIL

Round 1: With Color A, make a magic ring, 8 sc in ring. (8 sc)

Round 2: Inc in each st around. (16 sc)

Rounds 3-4: *(2 rounds)* Sc in each st around. (16 sc)

Stuff Tail.

Round 5: [Dec] 8 times. (8 sc)

Fasten off and weave in end. Alternatively, crochet over end when Tail attached to Body.

ARM (Make 2)

Round 1: With Color A, make a magic ring, 6 sc in ring. (6 sc)

Round 2: Inc in each st around. (12 sc)

Rounds 3-4: *(2 rounds)* Sc in each st around. (12 sc)

Round 5: [Dec] 3 times, sc in each of next 6 sts. (9 sc)

Start to stuff Arm and continue to stuff as you go. Stuff lower 2/3 of Arm only.

Rounds 6-9: *(4 rounds)* Sc in each st around. (9 sc)

Closing Row: Flatten Arm; working through both layers *(to close opening)*, sc in each of next 4 sts. (4 sc)

Fasten off and weave in end. Alternatively, crochet over end when Leg is attached to Body.

LEG (Make 2)

Round 1: With Color C, make a magic ring, 8 sc in ring. (8 sc)

Round 2: Inc in each st around. (16 sc)

Change to MC.

Round 3: Sc in each of next 4 sts, inc in each of next 8 sts, sc in each of next 4 sts. (24 sc)

Rounds 4-5: *(2 rounds)* Sc in each st around. (24 sc)

Round 6: Sc in each of next 4 sts, [sc in each of next 2 sts, dec] 4 times, sc in each of next 4 sts. (20 sc)

Round 7: Sc in each of next 4 sts, [sc in next st, dec] 4 times, sc in each of next 4 sts. (16 sc)

Round 8: Sc in each of next 2 sts, [dec, sc in next st] 4 times, sc in each of next 2 sts. (12 sc) Stuff Leg.

Round 9: Sc in each of next 2 sts, [dec] 4 times, sc in each of next 2 sts (8 sc)

> ### Orientation Check Point
> Flatten the top of the Leg so that the decreases are pointing upwards. You want the end of round to be to one side of the flattened end. If needed, work additional single crochet stitches to move the end of round to the side of the Leg.

Closing Row: Flatten Leg, ch 1; working through both layers *(to close opening)*, sc in each of next 4 sts. (4 sc)

Fasten off and weave in end. Alternatively, crochet over end when Leg is attached to Body.

HEAD

Round 1: With MC, make a magic ring, 8 sc in ring. (8 sc)

Round 2: Inc in each st around. (16 sc)

Rounds 3-4: *(2 rounds)* Sc in each st around. (16 sc)

Round 5: Sc in each of next 4 sts; change to Color A, hdc-inc in each of next 3 sts; change to MC, hdc-inc in each of next 2 sts; change to Color A, hdc-inc in each of next 3 sts; change to MC, sc in each of next 4 sts. (8 sc & 16 hdc)

PM on 2 middle hdc-sts *(marks center of Head and will help with orientation)*.

Round 6: Sc in each of next 4 sts; change to Color A, [sc in next st, inc in next st] 3 times; change to MC, sc in next st, inc in each of next 2 sts, sc in next st; change to Color A, [inc in next st, sc in next st] 3 times; change to MC, sc in each of next 4 sts. (32 sc)

Round 7: Sc in each of next 4 sts, [inc in next st, sc in each of next 2 sts] 4 times, [sc in each of next 2 sts, inc in next st] 4 times, sc in each of next 4 sts. (40 sc)

Round 8: Sc in each of next 4 sts, [sc in each of next 3 sts, inc in next st] 4 times, [inc in next st, sc in each of next 3 sts] 4 times, sc in each of next 4 sts. (48 sc)

Cut Color A and secure end.

Rounds 9-11: *(3 rounds)* Sc in each st around. (48 sc) *(image 1)*

> ### Orientation Check Point
> At the start of Round 13 you will make the opening for the Body, which is 8 stitches wide. This should be centered at the base of the Head. The start of round may change between Rounds 12 and 13 to allow for this (Round 12 may end before or after the current start of round).

Round 12: Sc in each st until you are 4 sts away from center base of Head; end round here. (48 sc)

Note: In the next round, you will attach the Ears. When attaching each Ear, flatten the last round of the Ear and hold it against the next stitches on the Head. Work the "attaching" stitches through both layers of the Ear and the Head together, across all three layers.

Round 13: Ch 8; move start of round marker to first ch; skip next 8 sts *(Body opening)*, sc in each of next 12 sts; *(Attach First Ear)* working on First Ear & Head, sc in each of next 3 sts; working on Head only, sc in each of next 10 sts; *(Attach Second Ear)* working on Second Ear & Head, sc in each of next 3 sts; working on Head only, sc in each of next 12 sts. (40 sc & 8 ch-sts) *(images 2-4)*

Round 14: Working in ch-8, sc in each of next 8 ch; sc in each remaining st around. (48 sc)

Rounds 15-16: *(2 rounds)* Sc in each st around. (48 sc)

Do not fasten off.

Face Details

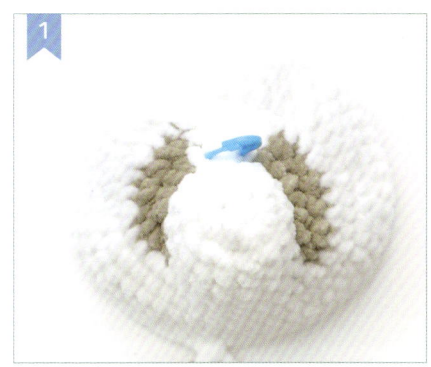

1. Add safety eyes centrally in the Color A patches on either side of the face.

2. With Color C, embroider small straight stitches to create cheeks on the lower outer aspects of the eyes.

3. With MC, embroider small highlights on outer aspects of safety eyes (optional).

4. With black thread, embroider small Eyebrows 2 rounds above the safety eyes.

5. With Color B, embroider the Nose, starting through the magic ring and continuing over the 2 rounds above, forming a triangular shape. Make one long horizontal stitch across the top of the nose, then make a vertical stitch down from the bottom of the Nose. *(images 5 -7)*

Stuff Head and continue to stuff as you go. Continue with Head.

Round 17: [Sc in each of next 4 sts, dec] 8 times. (40 sc)

Round 18: [Sc in each of next 3 sts, dec] 8 times. (32 sc)

Round 19: [Sc in each of next 2 sts, dec] 8 times. (24 sc)

Round 20: [Sc in next st, dec] 8 times. (16 sc)

Round 21: [Dec] 8 times. (8 sc)

Fasten off, leaving a long tail for sewing. Use yarn needle to weave yarn tail through front loops of final round and pull to close.

BODY

Note: In the next round, you will be working around the Body opening made in Round 13 of the Head, starting in the ch-8. To make starting the Body easier, remove some stuffing from Body opening. The stitch markers in the photos mark the corner spaces of Body opening. (image 8)

Round 1: Attach Color A at center back of Body opening *(4 ch-sts away from next corner space)*, sc in same ch, sc in each of next 3 ch, sc in next corner space between rounds, sc in each of next 8 sts, sc in next corner space between rounds, sc in each of next 4 ch. (18 sc) *(images 9 & 10)*

Round 2: [Sc in each of next 2 sts, inc in next st] 6 times. (24 sc)

> **Orientation Check Point**
> The next round should start centrally at the back of the Body. If needed, move the start of round forward (by making additional single crochet stitches), or back (by removing single crochet stitches) to allow for this. If you need to remove stitches that include an increase, make sure you remake the increase so you continue to have the correct stitch count.

Note: In the next round, you will attach the Arms. When attaching each Arm, hold the closing stitches of the Arm against the next stitches on the Body with the decreases of the Arm facing outwards. Work the "attaching" stitches through the Arm and the Body together, across both layers.

Round 3: Sc in each of next 4 sts; *(Attach First Arm)* working on First Arm & Body, sc in each of next 4 sts; working on Body only, sc in each of next 8 sts; *(Attach Second Arm)* working on Second Arm & Body, sc in each of next 4 sts; working on Body only, sc in each of next 4 sts. (24 sc) *(images 11 & 13)*

Round 4: [Sc in each of next 3 sts, inc in next st] 6 times. (30 sc)

Rounds 5-6: *(2 rounds)* Sc in each st around. (30 sc)

Change to MC. Cut Color A and secure end.

Round 7: [Sc in each of next 4 sts, inc in next st] 6 times. (36 sc)

Round 8: [Sc in each of next 5 sts, inc in next st] 6 times. (42 sc)

Rounds 9-12: *(4 rounds)* Sc in each st around. (42 sc)

> **Orientation Check Point**
> The next round should start centrally at the back of the Body. If needed, move the start of round forward (by making additional single crochet stitches), or back (by removing single crochet stitches) to allow for this.

Note: Over the next two rounds, you will attach the Tail (half at the end of Round 13 and half at the start of Round 14). When attaching the Tail, flatten the last round of the Tail and hold it against the next stitches on the Body. Work the "attaching" stitches through both layers of the Tail and the Body together, across all three layers.

Round 13: Sc in each of next 40 sts; *(Attach Tail)* working on Tail & Body, sc in each of next 2 sts. (42 sc) *(images 14 & 15)*

Round 14: *(Continue to Attach Tail)* Working on Tail & Body, sc in each of next 2 sts; working on Body only, sc in each of next 3 sts, dec, [sc in each of next 5 sts, dec] 5 times (36 sc)

Stuff Body and continue to stuff as you go.

Round 15: [Sc in each of next 4 sts, dec] 6 times. (30 sc)

Round 16: [Sc in each of next 3 sts, dec] 6 times. (24 sc)

> **Orientation Check Point**
> The next round should start centrally at the back of the Body. If needed, move the start of round forward (by making additional single crochet stitches), or back (by removing single crochet stitches) to allow for this. If you need to remove stitches that include a decrease, make sure you remake the decrease so you continue to have the correct stitch count.

Note: In the next round, you will attach the Legs. When attaching each Leg, hold the closing stitches of the Leg against the next stitches on the Body so that the foot points towards the front of the Panda once attached. Work each "attaching" stitch through the Leg and the Body together, across both layers.

Round 17: Sc in each of next 6 sts; *(Attach First Leg)* working on First Leg & Body, sc in each of next 4 sts; working on Body only, sc in each of next 4 sts; *(Attach Second Leg)* working on Second Leg & Body, sc in each of next 4 sts; working on Body only, sc in each of next 6 sts. (24 sc) *(images 16 & 17)*

Round 18: [Sc in next st, dec] 8 times. (16 sc)

Round 19: [Dec] 8 times. (8 sc)

Fasten off, leaving a long tail for sewing. Use yarn needle to weave yarn tail through front loops of final round and pull to close.

BABY PANDA

HEAD

Round 1: With MC, make a magic ring, 8 sc in ring. (8 sc)

Round 2: Inc in each st around. (16 sc)

Round 3: Sc in each of next 2 sts, inc in each of next 4 sts, sc in each of next 4 sts, inc in each of next 4 sts, sc in each of next 2 sts. (24 sc)

Round 4: Sc in each of next 5 sts; change to Color A, puff in next st; change to MC, sc in each of next 12 sts; change to Color A, puff in next st; change to MC, sc in each of next 5 sts. (22 sc & 2 puff-sts) *(image 18)*

Round 5: Sc in each of next 2 sts, [sc in next st, inc in next st] 4 times, sc in each of next 4 sts, [inc in next st, sc in next st] 4 times, sc in each of next 2 sts. (32 sc)

Round 6: Sc in each st around. (32 sc)

Round 7: Sc in each of next 2 sts, [sc in each of next 2 sts, inc in next st] 4 times, sc in each of next 4 sts, [inc in next st, sc in each of next 2 sts] 4 times, sc in each of next 2 sts. (40 sc)

Round 8: Sc in each st around. (40 sc)

> ### Orientation Check Point
> The next two stitches (those worked in the back loops only) should sit centrally at the back of the Head. If needed, move the start of round forward (by making additional single crochet stitches), or back (by removing single crochet stitches) to allow for this.

Round 9: Working in **back loops** only, sc in each of next 2 sts; PM on each unworked front loop; working in both loops, sc in each remaining st around. (40 sc)

Round 10: Sc in each st around. (40 sc)

Note: In the next round, you will make the opening for the Body.

Round 11: Ch 4; move start of round marker to first ch; skip next 4 sts *(Body opening)*, sc in each remaining st around. (36 sc & 4 ch-sts) *(image 19)*

Round 12: Working in ch-4, sc in each of next 4 ch; sc in each remaining st around. (40 sc)

Do not fasten off.

Face Details

1. Insert safety eyes on the front of the Head (the Body opening and two marked front loops are on the back) between Rounds 9 -10, approximately 10 sts apart (roughly in line with puff-sts).

2. With Color C, embroider a nose with horizontal straight stitches 4 sts wide between the Eyes.

3. With Color C, embroider small Cheeks between Rounds 10 &11 on either side of the Eyes.

4. With Color A, embroider a diagonal line on the lower outer aspect of each Eye. *(image 20)*

Continue with Head.

> ### Orientation Check Point
> The next round should start centrally at the back of the Head, in line with the center of the Body opening created in Round 11. If needed, move the start of round forward (by making additional single crochet stitches), or back (by removing single crochet stitches) to allow for this.

Round 13: Sc in each of next 2 sts, [sc in each of next 2 sts, dec] 4 times, sc in each of next 4 sts, [dec, sc in each of next 2 sts] 4 times, sc in each of next 2 sts. (32 sc)

Round 14: Sc in each of next 2 sts, [sc in next st, dec] 4 times, sc in each of next 4 sts, [dec, sc in next st] 4 times, sc in each of next 2 sts. (24 sc)

Stuff Head.

Round 15: [Sc in next st, dec] 8 times. (16 sc)

Round 16: [Dec] 8 times. (8 sc)

Fasten off, leaving a long tail for sewing. Use yarn needle to weave yarn tail through front loops of final round and pull to close. *(image 21)*

BODY

Note: In the next round, you will be working around the Body opening made in Round 11 of the Head, starting in the ch-4. The green stitch markers in photos mark the corner spaces of Body opening. (images 22 - 24)

Round 1: With the ears pointing away from you, attach Color A to far right ch *(of ch-4 from Round 11)* of Body opening, sc in same ch, sc in each of next 3 ch, inc in next corner space between rounds, inc in each of next 4 sts, inc in next corner space between rounds. (16 sc)

Round 2: Sc in each of next 4 sts, puff in next st, inc in next st, [sc in next st, inc in next st] 4 times, inc in next st, puff in next st. (20 sc & 2 puff-sts)

Note: In the next round, you will anchor the Head to the Body, through the marked unworked front loops of the Head. When anchoring the Head, hold the two marked front loops on Round 8 of the Head against the next stitches on the Body. Work the "attaching" stitches through the Head and the Body together, across both layers.

Round 3: Sc in each of next 4 sts, [sc in each of next 2 sts, inc in next st] 2 times, sc in each of next 2 sts; *(Attach Head)* working on Head *(in marked front loops)* & Body, inc in next st, sc in next st; working on Body only, sc in next st, inc in next st, [sc in each of next 2 sts, inc in next st] 2 times. (28 sc) *(images 25 - 27)*

Rounds 4-5: *(2 rounds)* Sc in each st around. (28 sc)

Change to MC.

Rounds 6-9: *(4 rounds)* Sc in each st around. (28 sc)

Orientation Check Point
The next round should start centrally on the underside of the Body. The first puff stitch made will be the Tail. If needed, move the start of round forward (by making additional single crochet stitches), or back (by removing single crochet stitches) to allow for this.

Round 10: Sc in each of next 14 sts; change to Color A, puff in next st; change to MC, sc in each of next 9 sts; change to Color A, puff in next st; change to MC, sc in each of next 3 sts. (26 sc & 2 puff-sts)

Round 11: Sc in each of next 3 sts; change to Color A, puff in next st; change to MC, [dec, sc in each of next 3 sts] 2 times, [sc in each of next 3 sts, dec] 2 times, sc in each of next 4 sts. (23 sc & 1 puff) *(image 28)*

Stuff Body.

Round 12: [Sc in next st, dec] 8 times. (16 sc)

Round 13: [Dec] 8 times. (8 sc)

Fasten off, leaving a long tail for sewing. Use yarn needle to weave yarn tail through front loops of final round and pull to close. *(image 29)*

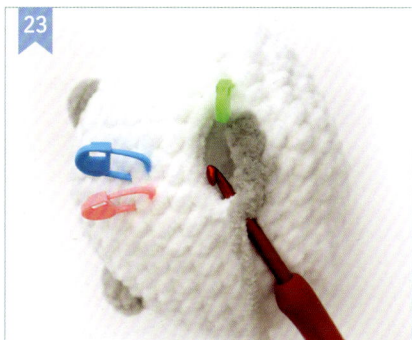
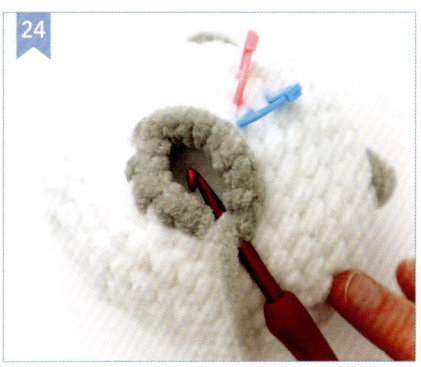

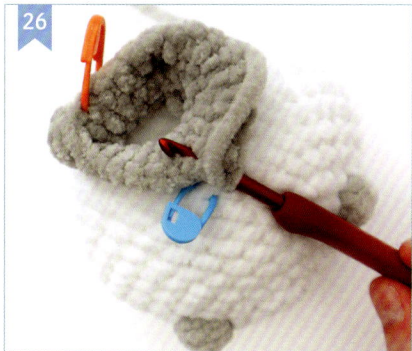

JAKE THE PUPPY

Like most puppies, Jake loves to chew things. He likes the new rope toy, but it isn't quite as good as a pair of fluffy slippers.

Skill Level: Intermediate
Sewing Level: No-sew

Finished Size: 28 cm

Yarn:

Hobbii Honey Bunny (3.5 oz, 131 yds/100 g, 120 m)

Main Color (MC): Silver (118) for Head, Front Legs, Body & Back Legs - 2 balls

Color A: Black (124) for Ears, Tail & Nose - 1 ball

Hobbii Toucan (3.5 oz, 131 yds/100 g, 120 m)

Color B: Cotton Candy (16) for Dog Toy & Cheeks – small amount

Color C: Mint (27) for Dog Toy – small amount

Color D: Sky Blue (21) for Dog Toy - small amount

Materials:

G-6 (4.00 mm) hook

Two 8 mm oval safety eyes

Stuffing

Stitch markers

Yarn needle

Scissors

White fingering weight cotton yarn – small amount (ex. Hobbii Friends 8/4 Cotton)

Orientation Check Points

Read these instructions carefully prior to starting the next round. You may be asked to alter the position of the start of the round before continuing.

EAR (Make 2)

Note: The ears are worked in rows.

Row 1: With Color A, ch 2, inc in 2nd ch from hook. (2 sc)

Row 2: Ch 1, turn, sc in each st across. (2 sc)

Row 3: Ch 1, turn, inc in each st across. (4 sc)

Row 4: Ch 1, turn, sc in each st across. (4 sc)

Row 5: Ch 1, turn, inc in next st, sc in each of next 2 sts, inc in next st. (6 sc)

Row 6: Ch 1, turn, sc in each st across. (6 sc)

Row 7: Ch 1, turn, inc in next st, sc in each of next 4 sts, inc in next st. (8 sc)

Row 8: Ch 1, turn, sc in each st across. (8 sc)

Edging: Ch 1, sc around all edges of Ear, making 3 sc in each corner.

Fasten off and weave in end. Alternatively, crochet over end when Ear attached to Head. *(image 1)*

TAIL

Round 1: With Color A, make a magic ring, 6 sc in ring. (6 sc)

Rounds 2-7: *(6 rounds)* Sc in each st around. (6 sc)

Do not stuff.

Closing Row: Flatten Tail, ch 1; working through both layers *(to close opening)*, sc in each of next 3 sts. (3 sc)

Fasten off and weave in end. Alternatively, crochet over end when Tail attached to Body.

HEAD

Round 1: With MC, make a magic ring, 8 sc in ring. (8 sc)

Round 2: Inc in each st around. (16 sc)

Round 3: [Sc in next st, inc in next st] 8 times. (24 sc)

Rounds 4-6: *(3 rounds)* Sc in each st around. (24 sc)

Round 7: Sc in each of next 8 sts, hdc-inc in each of next 8 sts, sc in each of next 8 sts. (16 sc & 16 hdc) PM on 2 middle hdc-sts *(marks center of Head and will help with orientation)*.

Round 8: Sc in each of next 8 sts, [sc in next st, inc in next st] 8 times, sc in each of next 8 sts. (40 sc)

Rounds 9-11: *(3 rounds)* Sc in each st around. (40 sc)

> **Orientation Check Point**
> The next round should start centrally at the base of the Head (directly opposite the marked central increase sts in Round 7). If needed, move the start of round forward (by making additional single crochet stitches), or back (by removing single crochet stitches) to allow for this.

Note: *In the next round, you will attach the Ears. When attaching each Ear, hold the base of the Ear against the next stitches on the Head. Work the "attaching" stitches through the Ear and the Head together, across both layers.*

Round 12: Sc in each of next 10 sts; *(Attach First Ear)* working on First Ear & Head, sc in each of next 8 sts; working on Head only, sc in each of next 4 sts; *(Attach Second Ear)* working on Second Ear & Head, sc in each of next 8 sts; working on Body only, sc in each of next 10 sts. (40 sc) *(images 2 - 5)*

Do not fasten off.

Face Details

1. With Color A, embroider the Nose over Rounds 2-4 of the Head in a triangular shape. Make one long horizontal stitch across the top of the Nose, then make a vertical line down from the bottom of the Nose, over 2 rounds.

2. Insert safety eyes on either side of the half double crochet increases from Round 7.

3. With white fingering weight cotton yarn, embroider small highlights on the outer aspects of the safety eyes (optional).

4. With Color B, embroider small cheeks.

Continue with Head.

Rounds 13-14: *(2 rounds)* Sc in each st around. (40 sc)

Round 15: [Sc in each of next 3 sts, dec] 8 times. (32 sc)

Stuff Head.

Round 16: [Sc in each of next 2 sts, dec] 8 times. (24 sc)

> **Orientation Check Point**
> In the next round, you will create the opening for the Body. The round should start centrally at the base of the Head. If needed, move the start of round forward (by making additional single crochet stitches), or back (by removing single crochet stitches) to allow for this. If you need to remove stitches that include a decrease, make sure you remake the decrease so you continue to have the correct stitch count.

Round 17: Sc in each of next 3 sts, [sc in next st, dec] 6 times, ch 4, skip next 6 sts *(Body opening;* **this will extend beyond end of round)**. *(image 6)*

Note: *The next stitch you make will be the new start of round.*

Round 18: [Dec] 6 times; working in ch-4, [dec] 2 times. (8 sc)

Fasten off, leaving a long tail for sewing. Use yarn needle to weave yarn tail through front loops of final round and pull to close.

FRONT LEGS

First Front Leg

Round 1: With MC, make a magic ring, 8 sc in ring. (8 sc)

Round 2: Inc in each st around. (16 sc)

Round 3: [Sc in next st, inc in next st] 8 times. (24 sc)

Rounds 4-6: *(3 rounds)* Sc in each st around. (24 sc)

Round 7: Sc in each of next 6 sts, [dec] 6 times, sc in each of next 6 sts. (18 sc)

Round 8: Sc in each of next 5 sts, [dec] 4 times, sc in each of next 5 sts. (14 sc)

Stuff Front Leg and continue to stuff as you go.

Rounds 9-14: *(6 rounds)* Sc in each st around. (14 sc)

Fasten off.

Second Front Leg

Rounds 1-14: *(14 rounds)* Repeat Rounds 1-14 of First Front Leg; work additional sc to move the end of round to side of Second Front Leg.

Do not fasten off. Continue to join the Front Legs with a chain.

Round 15: *(Joining Front Legs)* From Second Front Leg, ch 4; working on First Front Leg, sc in st on inner side of Leg *(so feet face same direction)*, sc in each of next 13 sts; working in ch-4, sc in each of next 4 ch; working on Second Front Leg, sc in each of next 14 sts. (32 sc & 4 ch-sts) *(images 7 & 8)*

Round 16: Working in ch-4, sc in each of next 4 ch, sc in each of next 3 sts, [dec] 4 times, sc in each of next 10 sts, [dec] 4 times, sc in each of next 3 sts. (28 sc)

Note: In the next round, you will attach the Head. When attaching the Head, hold the 6 skipped single crochet stitches on the base of the Head against the next stitches on the front of the Front Legs. Work the "attaching" stitches through the Head (from inside to outside) and the Front Legs together, across both layers.

Round 17: Sc in each of next 6 sts, dec, sc in each of next 2 sts, dec, sc in next st; *(Attach Head)* working on Head *(in skipped sc stitches)* & Front Legs, sc in each of next 6 sts; working on Front Legs only, sc in next st, dec, sc in each of next 2 sts, dec, sc in each of next 2 sts. (24 sc) *(images 9 & 10)*

Note: In the next round, you will crochet into the remaining unworked stitches of the Head. The attaching stitches from the previous round and the slip stitches made in the next round (to prevent gaps) will not be worked into again and are not included in overall stitch count.

Round 18: Sc in each of next 11 sts, sl st across same 2 sts as first attaching st; working on Head, inc in next corner space *(marked by a stitch marker in photo)*; working in ch-4 on Head, sc in each of next 4 ch; inc in next corner space on Head *(marked by a stitch marker in photo)*; sl st across same 2 sts as last attaching st; working on Front Legs, sc in each of next 7 sts. (26 sc) *(images 11 - 14)*

Do not fasten off. Continue with Body.

BODY

Round 19: [Sc in each of next 6 sts, inc in next st, sc in each of next 5 sts, inc in next st] 2 times. (30 sc)

Round 20: [Sc in each of next 4 sts, inc in next st] 6 times. (36 sc)

Rounds 21-22: *(2 rounds)* Sc in each st around. (36 sc)

Round 23: [Sc in each of next 5 sts, inc in next st] 6 times. (42 sc)

Rounds 24-25: *(2 rounds)* Sc in each st around. (42 sc)

Round 26: [Sc in each of next 6 sts, inc in next st] 6 times. (48 sc)

Rounds 27-28: *(2 rounds)* Sc in each st around. (48 sc)

Orientation Check Point
In the next round, you will be making the openings for the Back Legs. The round should start centrally at the base of the Body. If needed, move the start of round forward (by making additional single crochet stitches), or back (by removing single crochet stitches) to allow for this.

Round 29: Sc in each of next 2 sts, ch 7, skip next 7 sts *(First Back Leg opening)*, sc in each of next 30 sts, ch 7, skip next 7 sts *(Second Back Leg opening)*, sc in each of next 2 sts. (34 sc & 14 ch-sts) *(image 15)*

Round 30: Sc in each of next 2 sts; working in ch-7, sc in each of next 7 ch; sc in each of next 30 sts; working in ch-7, sc in each of next 7 ch; sc in each of next 2 sts. (48 sc)

Round 31: [Sc in each of next 6 sts, dec] 6 times. (42 sc)

Stuff Body and continue to stuff as you go.

Orientation Check Point
The next round should start centrally at the base of the Body. If needed, move the start of round forward (by making additional single crochet stitches), or back (by removing single crochet stitches) to allow for this. If you need to remove stitches that include a decrease, make sure you remake the decrease so you continue to have the correct stitch count.

Note: In the next round, you will attach the Tail. When attaching the Tail, hold the closing stitches of the Tail against the next stitches on the Body. Work the "attaching" stitches through the Tail and the Body together, across both layers.

Round 32: Sc in each of next 2 sts, dec, [sc in each of next 5 sts, dec] 2 times, sc in next st; *(Attach Tail)* working on Tail & Body, sc in each of next 3 sts; working on Body only, sc in next st, dec, [sc in each of next 5 sts, dec] 2 times, sc in each of next 3 sts. (36 sc) *(image 16)*

Round 33: [Sc in each of next 4 sts, dec] 6 times. (30 sc)

Round 34: [Sc in each of next 3 sts, dec] 6 times. (24 sc)

Round 35: [Sc in each of next 2 sts, dec] 6 times. (18 sc)

Round 36: [Sc in next st, dec] 6 times. (12 sc)

Round 37: [Dec] 6 times. (6 sc)

Fasten off, leaving a long tail for sewing. Use yarn needle to weave yarn tail through front loops of final round and pull to close.

BACK LEG (Make 2 – one in each Back Leg opening)

Note: In the next round, you will be working around a Leg opening made in Round 29 of the Body, starting in the skipped stitches. The stitch markers in the photo mark the corner spaces of the Back Leg opening. (image 17)

Round 1: With Front Legs & Head pointing down, attach MC to skipped st from Round 29 of Body on lower right side of Back Leg opening, sc in same st, sc in each of next 6 sts, dec across next corner space *(marked with stitch marker in photo)* and next ch, sc in each of next 5 ch, dec across next ch and next corner space *(marked with stitch marker in photo)*. (14 sc)

Rounds 2-5: *(4 rounds)* Sc in each st around. (14 sc)

Note: In the next round, you will anchor the Back Leg to the Body. When anchoring the Back Leg, fold the Leg up towards the backend of the Body so that the next stitches on the Leg are against the Body. Work each "attaching" stitch through the two closest stitch holes on the Body (inside then outside) and into the next stitch on the Back Leg together, across both layers.

Round 6: Sc in each of next 9 sts; fold Back Leg towards backend of Body; *(Attach Back Leg)* working on Body & Back Leg, sc in each of next 4 sts; working on Back Leg only, sc in next st. (14 sc) *(images 18 - 21)*

Rounds 7-10: *(4 rounds)* Sc in each st around. (14 sc)

Round 11: Working in **front loops** only, sc in each of next 2 sts, inc in each of next 4 sts, sc in each of next 8 sts. (18 sc)

Round 12: Sc in each of next 3 sts, inc in each of next 6 sts, sc in each of next 9 sts. (24 sc)

Stuff Back Leg and continue to stuff as you go.

Rounds 13-15: *(3 rounds)* Sc in each st around. (24 sc)

Round 16: [Sc in next st, dec] 8 times. (16 sc)

Round 17: [Dec] 8 times. (8 sc)

Fasten off, leaving a long tail for sewing. Use yarn needle to weave yarn tail through front loops of final round and pull to close. *(image 22)*

DOG TOY

Strands (Make 9)

Make 3 strands in Color B, 3 strands in Color C, and 3 strands in Color D.

Row 1: Starting with a long tail, ch 30.

Fasten off, leaving a long tail.

Braiding

1. Tie all starting tails of Strands together.

2. Separate Strands into 3 sets of 3 strands and braid each set to form 3 separate braids.

3. Braid these three braids together to form a larger braid.

4. Tie finishing tails of Strands together in a knot.

5. Trim all ends. *(image 23)*

STELLA THE SHARK

Stella has a sweet tooth that's bigger than her dorsal fin. Sharks may not have the best reputation, but Stella is determined to make friends with all her fellow sea creatures. Perhaps she can win them over with some seaweed cupcakes or a big hug.

Skill Level: Intermediate
Sewing Level: Low-sew

Finished Size: 32 cm

Yarn:

Hobbii Honey Bunny (3.5 oz, 131 yds/100 g, 120 m)

Main Color (MC): Lapis Blue (93) for Fins, Head, Body & Tail - 1 ball

Color A: White (01) for Head & Body - 1 ball

Materials:

- G-6 (4.00 mm) hook
- Two 25 mm kawaii sinker safety eyes (alternatively, use 15 mm black safety eyes with a 25 mm diameter circle of colored felt behind)
- Stuffing
- Stitch markers
- Yarn needle
- Doll jointing needle
- Scissors
- Black embroidery floss
- Dental floss or white fingering weight cotton yarn (ex. Hobbii Friends 8/4 Cotton) – small amount
- Blush (optional)

Orientation Check Points

Read these instructions carefully prior to starting the next round. You may be asked to alter the position of the start of the round before continuing.

FIN (Make 2)

Note: The Fin is worked in rows starting with a magic ring. Do not join. Do not stuff.

Row 1: With MC, make a magic ring, 4 sc in ring. (4 sc)

Row 2: Ch 1, turn, inc in each st across. (8 sc)

Row 3: Ch 1, turn, [sc in next st, inc in next st] 4 times. (12 sc)

Row 4: Ch 1, turn, [sc in each of next 2 sts, inc in next st] 4 times. (16 sc)

Row 5: Ch 1, turn, sc in each of next 8 sts; fold Fin in half; working through both layers, sc in each of next 8 sts. *(image 1)*

Closing Edge: Working in sides of Rows and through both layers *(to close opening)*, inc in first space, sc 3 more times across. (5 sc) *(image 2)*

Fasten off and weave in end. Alternatively, crochet over end when Fin attached to Body. *(images 3 & 4)*

HEAD

Round 1: With MC, make a magic ring, 5 sc in ring. (5 sc)

Round 2: Inc in next st, sc in each of next 4 sts. (6 sc)

Round 3: Inc in each of next 2 sts, sc in each of next 4 sts. (8 sc)

121

Round 4: Sc in next st, inc in each of next 2 sts, sc in each of next 5 sts. (10 sc)

Round 5: Sc in each of next 2 sts, hdc-inc in each of next 2 sts, sc in each of next 6 sts. (8 sc & 4 hdc)

Round 6: Sc in each of next 3 sts, hdc-inc in each of next 2 sts, sc in each of next 7 sts. (10 sc & 4 hdc)

Round 7: Sc in each of next 4 sts, hdc-inc in each of next 2 sts, sc in each of next 8 sts. (12 sc & 4 hdc) PM on 2 middle hdc-sts *(marks center of Head and will help with orientation)*. *(image 5)*

Round 8: [Sc in next st, inc in next st] 8 times. (24 sc)

Round 9: [Sc in each of next 2 sts, inc in next st] 8 times. (32 sc)

Round 10: [Sc in each of next 3 sts, inc in next st] 8 times. (40 sc)

Round 11: [Sc in each of next 4 sts, inc in next st] 8 times. (48 sc)

Rounds 12-17: *(6 rounds)* Sc in each st around. (48 sc)

> **Orientation Check Point**
> The next round should start centrally at the back of the Head (directly opposite the marked central hdc-sts in Round 7). If needed, move the start of round forward (by making additional single crochet stitches), or back (by removing single crochet stitches) to allow for this.

Round 18: Sc in each of next 16 sts, [hdc in next st, hdc-inc in next st] 8 times, sc in each of next 16 sts. (32 sc & 24 hdc)

Change to Color A

Rounds 19-23: *(5 rounds)* Sc in each st around. (56 sc)

> **Orientation Check Point**
> The next round should start centrally at the back of the Head. If needed, move the start of round forward (by making additional single crochet stitches), or back (by removing single crochet stitches) to allow for this.

Round 24: Sc in each of next 12 sts, [hdc in next st, hdc-dec] 8 times, sc in each of next 20 sts. (32 sc & 16 hdc)

Round 25: [Sc in each of next 4 sts, dec] 8 times. (40 sc)

Round 26: [Sc in each of next 3 sts, dec] 8 times. (32 sc)

Do not fasten off.

Face Details

1. Insert safety eyes between Rounds 16 & 17 with 12 sts between them. The eyes should be centered with the hdc-sts of Round 18.

2. Stuff Head firmly.

3. With Color A, embroider small highlights on the lower outer aspects of the safety eyes.

4. With black embroidery floss, embroider oblique lines over the top of the safety eyes. *(image 6)*

5. With white fingering weight cotton yarn or dental floss and doll jointing needle, add facial shaping. Bring your needle from inside the head to out near the lower inner corner of the shark's right eye. Insert the needle into the stitch hole above your position and then out at the upper inner corner of the shark's left eye. Insert your needle in through the stitch hole below your position and then out at the center front of the Head at Round 23. Insert your needle back inside the Head one stitch horizontally over from your current position. Both of your thread ends should be inside the Head now. Pull the ends tightly to draw in the eyes and create an indent for the mouth. Tie the ends together to secure them. *(images 7 - 12)*

6. With black embroidery floss, embroider gills over Rounds 17-19 on both sides of the face.

7. Add blush for cheeks (optional).

Continue with Head.

Round 27: [Sc in each of next 2 sts, dec] 8 times. (24 sc)

Round 28: Sc in each st around until you reach the center back of Head. (24 sc)

Do not fasten off. Continue to Body.

BODY

Change to MC.

Round 29: [Sc in each of next 2 sts, inc in next st] 2 times; change to Color A, [sc in each of next 2 sts, inc in next st] 4 times; change to MC, [sc in each of next 2 sts, inc in next st] 2 times. (32 sc)

Round 30: Sc in each of next 10 sts; change to Color A, sc in each of next 12 sts; change to MC, sc in each of next 10 sts. (32 sc)

Round 31: Sc in each of next 12 sts; change to Color A, sc in each of next 8 sts; change to MC, sc in each of next 12 sts. (32 sc)

Note: In the next round, you will attach the Fins. When attaching each Fin, hold the closing stitches of the Fin against the next stitches on the Body with the curve of the Fin towards the front of the Shark. Work the "attaching" stitches through the Fin and the Body together, across both layers.

Round 32: Sc in each of next 5 sts; *(Attach First Fin)* working on First Fin & Body, sc in each of next 5 sts; working on Body only, sc in each of next 4 sts; change to Color A, sc in each of next 4 sts on Body; change to MC, sc in each of next 4 sts on Body; *(Attach Second Fin)* working on Second Fin & Body, sc in each of next 5 sts; working on Body only, sc in each of next 5 sts. (32 sc) *(images 13 & 14)*

Round 33: [Sc in each of next 3 sts, inc in next st] 3 times, sc in each of next 3 sts; sc in next st; change to Color A, sc in same st as last sc, sc in next st; change to

MC, sc in each of next 2 sts, inc in next st, [sc in each of next 3 sts, inc in next st] 3 times (40 sc)

Cut Color A and weave in end.

Rounds 34-39: *(6 rounds)* Sc in each st around. (40 sc)

Start stuffing Body and continue to stuff as you go.

Round 40: [Sc in each of next 3 sts, dec] 8 times. (32 sc)

Rounds 41-42: *(2 rounds)* Sc in each st around. (32 sc)

Round 43: [Sc in each of next 2 sts, dec] 8 times. (24 sc)

Rounds 44-45: *(2 rounds)* Sc in each st around. (24 sc)

Round 46: [Sc in each of next 2 sts, dec] 6 times. (18 sc)

Round 47: Sc in each st around. (18 sc)

Round 48: [Sc in next st, dec] 6 times. (12 sc)

Orientation Check Point
The next round should start centrally at the back of the Body. If needed, move the start of round forward (by making additional single crochet stitches), or back (by removing single crochet stitches) to allow for this. If you need to remove stitches that include a decrease, make sure you remake the decrease so you continue to have the correct stitch count.

Do not fasten off. Continue to Tail.

TAIL

Tail Fin Openings: Ch 2, skip 6 sts. PM on first skipped st. *(image 15)*

First Tail Fin

Round 1: Sc in each of next 6 sts; working in ch-2, sc in each of next 2 ch. (8 sc)

Round 2: [Sc in each of next 2 sts, inc in each of next 2 sts] 2 times. (12 sc)

Round 3: Sc in each st around. (12 sc)

Round 4: Sc in each of next 3 sts, inc in each of next 2 sts, sc in each of next 4 sts, inc in each of next 2 sts, sc in next st. (16 sc)

Round 5: Sc in each of next 3 sts, [dec] 2 times, sc in each of next 4 sts, [dec] 2 times, sc in next st. (12 sc)

Round 6: Sc in each of next 2 sts, [dec] 2 times, sc in each of next 2 sts, [dec] 2 times. (8 sc)

Round 7: [Dec] 4 times. (4 sc)

Do not stuff. Flatten First Tail Fin.

Fasten off, leaving a long tail for sewing. Use yarn needle to weave yarn tail through front loops of final round and pull to close. *(image 16)*

Second Tail Fin

Attach MC to marked skipped stitch on Round 48 of Body (second Tail Fin opening) and remove marker. *(image 17)*

Rounds 1-7: *(7 rounds)* Repeat rounds 1-7 of First Tail Fin.

Do not stuff. Flatten Second Tail Fin.

Fasten off, leaving a long tail for sewing. Use yarn needle to weave yarn tail through front loops of final round and pull to close. *(image 18)*

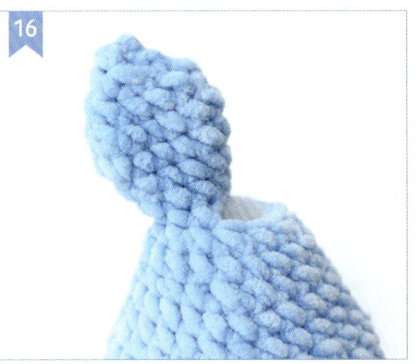

SATINSKY THE SWAN

Satinsky is the captain of the swan synchronized swimming team. He glides gracefully across the water and has led the team to many victories.

Skill Level: Intermediate
Sewing Level: No-sew

Finished Size: 24 cm

Yarn:

Hobbii Honey Bunny (3.5 oz, 131 yds/100 g, 120 m)

Main Color (MC): White (01) for Wings, Head, Neck & Body - 1 ball

Color A: Gold Dust (27) for Beak - 1 ball

Color B: Black (124) for Beak - small amounts only

Hobbii Peacock (3.5 oz, 71 yds/100 g, 65 m)

Color C: White (01) for Neck Fluff & Tail - 1 ball

Hobbii Toucan (3.5 oz, 131 yds/100 g, 120 m)

Color D: Cotton Candy (16) for Cheeks – small amount

Materials:

G-6 (4.00 mm) hook
Two 8 mm oval safety eyes
Stuffing
Stitch markers
Yarn needle
Scissors
Foam roller (optional)

Orientation Check Points

Read these instructions carefully prior to starting the next round. You may be asked to alter the position of the start of the round before continuing.

WINGS

Wing 1

Row 1: With MC, ch 11; sc in 2nd ch from hook, sc in each of next 7 ch; PM on unworked loop of last ch worked into; inc in each of next 2 ch. (12 sc)

Row 2: Ch 1, turn, inc in each of next 4 sts, sc in each of next 8 sts. (16 sc)

Row 3: Ch 1, turn; working in **back loops** only, sc in each of next 8 sts, inc in each of next 8 sts. (24 sc)

Row 4: Ch 1, turn, [sc in next st, inc in next st] 8 times, sc in each of next 8 sts. (32 sc)

Row 5: Turn, [ch 6, sl st in 2nd ch from hook, sl st in each of next 4 ch, sl st in next st on Row 4] 32 times. (32 feathers)

Fasten off and weave in end. *(image 1)*

With feathers of Row 5 pointing upwards and the starting ch-11 pointing downwards, attach MC to first (far right) unworked front loop of Row 2. *(image 2)*

Inner Row of Feathers: [Ch 6 sl st in 2nd ch from hook, sl st in each of next 4 ch, sl st in next unworked front loop on Wing] 16 times. (16 feathers)

Fasten off and weave in end. *(image 3)*

Wing 2

Rows 1-2: *(2 rows)* Repeat Rows 1-2 of Wing 1.

Row 3: Ch 1, turn; working in **front loops** only, sc in each of next 8 sts, inc in each of next 8 sts. (24 sc)

Rows 4-5: *(2 rows)* Repeat Rows 4-5 of Wing 1.

Fasten off and weave in end.

With feathers of Row 5 pointing upwards and the starting ch-11 pointing downwards, attach MC to first (far right) unworked back loop of Row 2.

Inner Row of Feathers: [Ch 6, sl st in 2nd ch from hook, sl st in each of next 4 ch, sl st in next unworked back loop on Wing] 16 times. (16 feathers)

Fasten off and weave in end.

Note: Your wings should look like mirror images of each other. Wing 1 will become the Swan's left wing and Wing 2 the right wing.

BEAK

Round 1: With Color A, ch 4, inc in 2nd ch from hook, sc in next ch, 3 sc in last ch; working on other side of starting ch, sc in each of next 2 ch. (8 sc)

Round 2: Sc in each st around. (8 sc)

Round 3: Sc in each of next 2 sts, inc in each of next 2 sts, sc in each of next 4 sts. (10 sc)

Round 4: [Sc in each of next 2 sts, inc in next st] 2 times, sc in each of next 4 sts. (12 sc)

Round 5: Sc in each of next 2 sts, [inc in next st, sc in each of next 4 sts] 2 times. (14 sc)

Round 6: Sc in each of next 2 sts, inc in next st; PM on first st of inc just made *(bright green st marker in photo)*, sc in each of next 6 sts, inc in next st, sc in each of next 4 sts. (16 sc)

Change to Color B

Round 7: Working in **front loops** only, sl st in each st around. (16 sl st)

Fasten off and weave in end. *(images 4 & 5)*

HEAD

Attach MC 4 sts before the marked stitch on Round 6 of Beak *(green stitch marker in photo)*. Remove marker.

Round 8: Working through **back loops** only of Color B sl sts and **back loops** only of Round 6 together, across both layers, for entire round, sc in each of next 4 sts, hdc-inc in each of next 8 sts, sc in each of next 4 sts. (8 sc & 16 hdc) PM on 2 middle hdc-sts *(marks center of Head and will help with orientation)*. *(image 6)*

Round 9: Sc in each of next 4 sts, [sc in next st, inc in next st] 4 times, [inc in next st, sc in next st] 4 times, sc in each of next 4 sts. (32 sc)

Rounds 10-14: *(5 rounds)* Sc in each st around. (32 sc)

Do not fasten off.

Face Details

1. Add safety eyes between Rounds 8 & 9 on either side of Beak.

2. With Color D, embroider small Cheeks on the lower outer aspects of the Eyes.

Continue with Head. *(image 7)*

Orientation Check Point

The next round should start centrally at the base of the Head (directly opposite the marked middle hdc-sts in Round 8). If needed, move the start of round forward (by making additional single crochet stitches), or back (by removing single crochet stitches) to allow for this.

Note: In the next round, you will make the opening for the Neck.

Round 15: Sc in each of next 29 sts, ch 6, skip next 6 sts *(Neck opening;* **this will extend beyond end of round***)*. (29 sc & 6 ch-sts) *(image 8)*

Note: The next stitch you make will be the new start of round.

Round 16: Sc in each of next 26 sts; working in ch-6, sc in each of next 6 ch. (32 sc)

Stuff Head.

Round 17: [Sc in each of next 2 sts, dec] 8 times. (24 sc)

Round 18: [Sc in next st, dec] 8 times. (16 sc)

Round 19: [Dec] 8 times. (8 sc)

Fasten off, leaving a long tail for sewing. Use yarn needle to weave yarn tail through front loops of final round and pull to close.

NECK

Note: In the next round, you will be working around the Neck opening made in Round 15 of the Head, starting in the ch-6. The stitch markers in the photos mark the corner spaces of Neck opening. (image 9)

Round 1: Attach MC at center back of Neck opening *(3 ch-sts away from next corner space)*, sc in same ch, sc in each of next 2 ch, inc in next corner space between rounds, sc in each of next 6 sts, inc in next corner space between rounds, sc in each of next 3 ch. (16 sc) *(image 10)*

Round 2: Hdc in each of next 4 sts, sc in each of next 8 sts, hdc in each of next 4 sts. (8 hdc & 8 sc)

Round 3: Sc in each st around. (16 sc)

Orientation Check Point

The next round should start centrally at the back of the Neck. If needed, move the start of round forward (by making additional single crochet stitches), or back (by removing single crochet stitches) to allow for this.

Note: In the next round, you will anchor the Head to the Neck. This will enhance the curve of the Neck. When anchoring the Head, hold the underside of the Head against the next stitches on the Neck (you will need to fold the Neck to meet the Head). Work each "attaching" stitch through the two closest stitch holes on the underside of the Head (inside then outside) and into the next stitch on the Neck together, across both layers.

Round 4: Hdc in each of next 4 sts, sc in each of next 3 sts; *(Attach Head)* working on Head & Neck, sc in each of next 2 sts; working on Neck only, sc in each of next 3 st, hdc in each of next 4 sts. (8 hdc & 8 sc) *(images 11 - 14)*

Insert foam roller (optional) and continue to work around it. The roller should reach into the base of the head.

Stuff Neck and continue to stuff as you go.

Round 5: Sc in each st around. (16 sc)

Round 6: Hdc in each of next 4 sts, sc in each of next 8 sts, hdc in each of next 4 sts. (8 hdc & 8 sc)

Round 7: Sc in each st around. (16 sc)

Round 8: Hdc in each of next 4 sts, sc in each of next 8 sts, hdc in each of next 4 sts. (8 hdc & 8 sc)

Round 9: Sc in each st around. (16 sc)

Round 10: Hdc in each of next 4 sts, sc in each of next 8 sts, hdc in each of next 4 sts. (8 hdc & 8 sc)

Rounds 11-13: *(3 rounds)* Sc in each st around. (16 sc)

Rounds 14-15: *(2 rounds)* Working in **back loops** only, sc in each st around. (16 sc)

Do not fasten off. Continue to Body.

BODY

Note: In the next round, you will form the Body by working around a chain. The end of round will extend beyond the start of round marker.

Round 16: Sc in next st, ch 8, inc in 2nd ch from hook, sc in each of next 6 ch, sl st in same st as first sc of round *(sl st will not be worked into again and is not included in overall st count)*, sc in each of next 15 sts on Neck; continuing beyond start of round, sc in next st; working on other side of ch-8, sc in each of next 6 ch, inc in last ch. (32 sc)

Note: The next stitch you make will be the new start of round. (image 15)

Round 17: Inc in each of next 2 sts, sc in each of next 6 sts, skip sl st from Round 16, [sc in each of next 3 sts, inc in next st] 4 times, sc in each of next 6 sts, inc in each of next 2 sts. (40 sc) *(image 16)*

Round 18: [Sc in next st, inc in next st] 2 times, sc in each of next 6 sts, [inc in next st, sc in each of next 4 sts] 4 times, sc in each of next 6 sts, [inc in next st, sc in next st] 2 times. (48 sc) *(image 17)*

Rounds 19-20: *(2 rounds)* Sc in each st around. (48 sc)

Orientation Check Point

In the next round, you will attach the Wings. Map out the position of each Wing before starting the round. Each Wing attaches to one side of the Body over 8 sts. There should be 14 sts between the Wings at the back of the body and 18 sts between the Wings at the front of the body. Using stitch markers, mark the positions of the first and last stitches of each Wing, with 6 stitches between each. *(images 18 & 19)*

Note: When attaching each Wing, you will work on the other side of the Wing's foundation chain, up to the stitch marker placed in Row 1 (8 ch-sts total). Hold the 8 ch-sts of the Wing against the next stitches on the Body with the feathers facing inwards and the curved part of the Wing pointing towards the back of the Body. Work the "attaching" stitches through the Wing and the Body together, across both layers. Which Wing you attach depends on which side of the Body you are on: Wing 1 is attached on the Swan's left side (pink stitch markers in photo) and Wing 2 is attached on the right side (green stitch markers in photo).

Round 21: Sc in each st until you reach stitch markers to Attach a Wing; *(Attach Wing)* working on Wing & Body, sc in each of next 8 sts; working on Body only, sc in each of next 18 sts; *(Attach Wing)* working on Wing & Body, sc in each next 8 sts; working on Body only, sc in each remaining st around. (48 sc) *(images 20 & 21)*

Rounds 22-24: *(3 rounds)* Sc in each st around. (48 sc)

Do not fasten off. Remove hook and place marker in working loop to secure it. Continue to Neck Fluff and then Tail.

NECK FLUFF

With Head pointing downwards, attach Color C to first unworked **front loop** of Round 13 of Neck. *(images 22 & 23)*

Rounds 1-2: *(2 rounds)* Working in unworked **front loops** only, [ch 3, sl st in next st] 16 times. (16 loops)

Fasten off. Pull the yarn tails inside the Neck and knot them together to secure.

TAIL

With Color C, insert your hook inside then outside (through two stitch holes) between Rounds 17 & 18 at the back of the Body, just to the right of center, and pull a loop through. *(images 24 - 26)*

Tail Loops: Ch 7, insert hook inside then outside through two stitch holes to the left and sl st, ch 10, insert hook inside then outside through two stitch holes to the left and sl st, ch 7, insert hook inside then outside through two stitch holes to the left and sl st. (3 loops)

Fasten off. Pull the yarn tails inside the Body and knot them together to secure.

Insert hook in marked working loop of Body and continue.

Orientation Check Point

The next round should start centrally at the tail end of the Body. If needed, move the start of round forward (by making additional single crochet stitches), or back (by removing single crochet stitches) to allow for this.

Round 25: Dec, sc in each of next 2 sts, dec, sc in each of next 36 sts, dec, sc in each of next 2 sts, dec. (44 sc)

Round 26: Sc in each of next 12 sts, [sc in each of next 3 sts, dec] 4 times, sc in each of next 12 sts (40 sc)

Orientation Check Point
The next round should start centrally at the tail end of the Body. If needed, move the start of round forward (by making additional single crochet stitches), or back (by removing single crochet stitches) to allow for this.

Round 27: [Sc in each of next 2 sts, dec] 2 times, sc in each of next 24 sts, [dec, sc in each of next 2 sts] 2 times. (36 sc)

Round 28: Sc in each st around. (36 sc) Stuff Body.

Round 29: Sc in each of next 12 sts, [sc in next st, dec] 4 times, sc in each of next 12 sts. (32 sc)

Round 30: Sc in each st around. (32 sc)

Round 31: [Sc in each of next 2 sts, dec] 8 times. (24 sc)

Round 32: [Sc in next st, dec] 8 times. (16 sc)

Round 33: [Dec] 8 times. (8 sc)

Fasten off, leaving a long tail for sewing. Use yarn tail to weave yarn tail through front loops of final round and pull to close.

TEACUP BUDDIES

Best friends Freddy and Hop love to share afternoon tea together. Their favorite is a cup of Earl Grey along with a shortbread biscuit for dipping.

Skill Level: Beginner
Sewing Level: No-sew

Finished Size:
Bunny 19 cm & Frog 17 cm

Yarn:

Rabbit: Hobbii Honey Bunny (3.5 oz, 131 yds/100 g, 120 m)

Main Color (MC-1): White (01) for Ears, Head & Body – 1 ball

Frog: Hobbii Honey Bunny (3.5 oz, 131 yds/100 g, 120 m)

Main Color (MC-2): Shamrock (104) for Eye Bumps, Head & Body – 1 ball

Accessories: Hobbii Honey Bunny (3.5 oz, 131 yds/100 g, 120 m)

Color A: Lilac (63) for Scarf & Outer Teacup – 1 ball

Color B: Turquoise (94) for Collar & Bow – 1 ball

Color C: Candyfloss (45) for Outer Teacup – 1 ball

Hobbii Honey Bunny Candy (3.5 oz, 131 yds/100 g, 120 m)

Color D: Beige (05) for Inner Teacup – 1 ball

Materials:

G-6 (4.00 mm) hook

Two 8 mm oval safety eyes

Stuffing

Yarn needle

Scissors

Embroidery Floss

White fingering weight cotton yarn – small amount (ex. Hobbii Friends 8/4 Cotton)

Blush (optional)

Orientation Check Points

Read these instructions carefully prior to starting the next round. You may be asked to alter the position of the start of the round before continuing.

Special Stitches:

Puff Stitch (puff):

Starting with a loop on your hook, yarn over and insert hook in the next stitch. Yarn over and pull a loop through (3 loops on hook). Yarn over and pull through 2 loops on hook (2 loops remain on hook). Repeat this process into the **same stitch** 4 more times (6 loops remain on hook). Yarn over and pull through all loops on hook.

RABBIT

EARS

First Ear

Round 1: With MC-1, make a magic ring, 6 sc in ring. (6 sc)

Round 2: [Sc in next st, inc in next st] 3 times. (9 sc)

Rounds 3-7: *(5 rounds)* Sc in each st around. (9 sc)

Stuff Ear. Fasten off.

Second Ear

Rounds 1-7: *(7 rounds)* Repeat Rounds 1-7 of First Ear.

Stuff Ear.

Do not fasten off. Continue with Head & Body to join the Ears together with a chain. *(image 1)*

HEAD & BODY

Round 8: *(Joining Ears)* Continuing from Second Ear, ch 1; working on First Ear, sc in next st; move start of round to st just made, sc in each of next 8 sts on First Ear; working in ch-1, inc in next ch; working on Second Ear, sc in each of next 9 sts; working on other side of ch-1, inc in next ch. (22 sc) *(images 2 - 6)*

Round 9: Sc in each of next 4 sts, inc in next st, sc in each of next 10 sts, inc in next st, sc in each of next 6 sts. (24 sc)

Round 10: Sc in next st, [sc in next st, inc in next st] 4 times, sc in each of next 4 sts, [sc in next st, inc in next st] 4 times, sc in each of next 3 sts. (32 sc)

Round 11: Sc in each st around. (32 sc)

Round 12: Sc in each of next 2 sts, [sc in each of next 2 sts, inc in next st] 4 times, sc in each of next 4 sts, [sc in each of next 2 sts, inc in next st] 4 times, sc in each of next 2 sts. (40 sc)

Rounds 13-17: *(5 rounds)* Sc in each st around. (40 sc)

Insert safety eyes in line with Ears between Rounds 11 & 12 with 6 stitches visible between them. *(image 7)*

Round 18: Sc in each of next 3 sts, [sc in each of next 2 sts, dec] 4 times, sc in each of next 4 sts, [sc in each of next 2 sts, dec] 4 times, sc in next st. (32 sc)

Round 19: Sc in each of next 3 sts, [sc in next st, dec] 4 times, sc in each of next 4 sts, [sc in next st, dec] 4 times, sc in next st. (24 sc)

Stuff Head and continue to stuff as you go.

Round 20: Sc in each of next 3 sts, [dec] 4 times, sc in each of next 4 sts, [dec] 4 times, sc in next st. (16 sc) *(image 8)*

Rounds 21-22: *(2 rounds)* Sc in each st around. (16 sc)

Round 23: Sc in each of next 6 sts, puff in next st, sc in each of next 6 sts, puff in next st, sc in each of next 2 sts. (14 sc & 2 puff-sts) *(image 9)*

Round 24: [Sc in each of next 3 sts, inc in next st] 4 times. (20 sc)

Rounds 25-27: *(3 rounds)* Sc in each st around. (20 sc)

Round 28: Dec, puff in next st, sc in next st, [dec, sc in each of next 2 sts] 4 times. (14 sc & 1 puff) *(image 10)*

Round 29: [Sc in next st, dec] 2 times, puff in next st, sc in next st, dec, sc in each of next 2 sts, puff in next st, sc in each of next 2 sts. (10 sc & 2 puff-sts) *(image 11)*

Round 30: [Dec] 6 times. (6 sc)

Fasten off, leaving a long tail for sewing. Use yarn needle to weave yarn tail through front loops of final round and pull to close.

1. With black embroidery floss, embroider a small Mouth between the safety eyes.

2. Add Cheeks using blush (optional).

FROG

EYE BUMPS

First Eye Bump

Round 1: With MC-2, make a magic ring, 6 sc in ring. (6 sc)

Round 2: [Sc in next st, inc in next st] 3 times. (9 sc)

Rounds 3-4: *(2 rounds)* Sc in each st around. (9 sc)

Fasten off.

Second Eye Bump

Rounds 1-4: *(4 rounds)* Repeat Rounds 1-4 of First Eye Bump.

Do not fasten off. Continue with Head & Body.

HEAD & BODY

Round 5: *(Joining Eye Bumps)* Continuing from Second Eye Bump, ch 1; working on First Eye Bump, sc in next st; move start of round to st just made, sc in each of next 8 sts on First Eye Bump; working in ch-1, inc in next ch; working on Second Ear, sc in each of next 9 sts; working on other side of ch-1, inc in next ch. (22 sc)

Round 6: Sc in each of next 4 sts, inc in next st, sc in each of next 10 sts, inc in next st, sc in each of next 6 sts. (24 sc)

Round 7: Sc in next st, [sc in next st, inc in next st] 4 times, sc in each of next 4 sts, [sc in next st, inc in next st] 4 times, sc in each of next 3 sts. (32 sc)

Round 8: Sc in each st around. (32 sc)

Round 9: Sc in each of next 2 sts, [sc in each of next 2 sts, inc in next st] 4 times, sc in each of next 4 sts, [sc in each of next 2 sts, inc in next st] 4 times, sc in each of next 2 sts. (40 sc)

Rounds 10-14: *(5 rounds)* Sc in each st around. (40 sc)

Do not fasten off.

Face Details

1. Insert safety eyes on the opposite side to the start of the round between Rounds 4 & 5 at the base of the eye bumps.

2. With white yarn, embroider small highlights on the outer aspects of the eyes.

3. With black embroidery floss, embroider a small smile over Round 5 between the Eyes.

4. Add Cheeks using blush (optional).

Continue with Head & Body.

Round 15: Sc in each of next 3 sts, [sc in each of next 2 sts, dec] 4 times, sc in each of next 4 sts, [sc in each of next 2 sts, dec] 4 times, sc in next st. (32 sc)

Round 16: Sc in each of next 3 sts, [sc in next st, dec] 4 times, sc in each of next 4 sts, [sc in next st, dec] 4 times, sc in next st. (24 sc)

Stuff Head and continue to stuff as you go.

Round 17: Sc in each of next 3 sts, [dec] 4 times, sc in each of next 4 sts, [dec] 4 times, sc in next st. (16 sc)

Rounds 18-19: *(2 rounds)* Sc in each st around. (16 sc)

Round 20: Sc in each of next 6 sts, puff in next st, sc in each of next 6 sts, puff in next st, sc in each of next 2 sts. (14 sc & 2 puff-sts)

Round 21: [Sc in each of next 3 sts, inc in next st] 4 times. (20 sc)

Rounds 22-24: *(3 rounds)* Sc in each st around. (20 sc)

Round 25: [Dec, sc in each of next 2 sts] 5 times. (15 sc)

Round 26: [Sc in next st, dec] 2 times, puff in next st, sc in next st, dec, sc in each of next 2 sts, puff in next st, sc in each of next 2 sts. (10 sc & 2 puff-sts)

Round 27: [Dec] 6 times. (6 sc)

Fasten off and weave in end.

ACCESSORIES

Note: These can be used interchangeably for the Frog or Rabbit.

SCARF

Row 1: With Color A, ch 39, sc in 2nd ch from hook, sc in each of next 37 ch. (38 sc)

Fasten off and weave in end.

COLLAR

With Color B, ch 21. Fasten off.

BOW

Row 1: With Color B, ch 22, hdc in 3rd ch from hook, hdc in each of next 19 ch. (20 hdc)

Rows 2-4: *(3 rows)* Ch 2, turn; working in **back loops** only, hdc in each st across. (20 hdc) Do not fasten off.

Edging: Ch 1, sc around all edges, making an inc in each corner as you go. Do not fasten off.

Cinch: Sl st in each st until you reach halfway along one long edge, ch 4; wrap ch-4 around center of Bow and around Collar; sl st in first ch to form a ring.

1. Wrap the Collar around the neck and secure the ends together.

2. Slide the Bow to the back of the neck. *(images 12 -20)*

TEACUP

Inner layer

Round 1: With Color D, make a magic ring, 6 sc in ring. (6 sc)

Round 2: Inc in each st around. (12 sc)

Round 3: [Sc in next st, inc in next st] 6 times. (18 sc)

Round 4: [Sc in each of next 2 sts, inc in next st] 6 times. (24 sc)

Round 5: [Sc in each of next 3 sts, inc in next st] 6 times. (30 sc)

Rounds 6-8: *(3 rounds)* Sc in each st around. (30 sc)

Fasten off and weave in end. *(image 21)*

Outer layer

Rounds 1-8: *(8 rounds)* With Color A or C, repeat Rounds 1-8 of Inner Layer.

Rounds 9-11: *(3 rounds)* Sc in each st around. (30 sc)

Note: In the next round you will attach the Inner Layer to the Outer Layer. Place the Inner Layer inside the Outer Layer with both wrong sides facing inwards. Work the "attaching" stitches through the Outer Layer and Inner Layer together, across both layers.

Round 12: (Attach Inner Layer) Working on Outer Layer & Inner Layer, sc in each st around. (30 sc) *(images 22 & 23)*

Handle: Ch 8, insert your hook inside then outside through two stitch holes between Rounds 6 & 7 on Outer Layer, pull a loop through, ch 1; working in ch-8, sl st in next ch, sc in each of next 7 ch, sl st back into Round 12 of Cup.

Fasten off and weave in end. *(images 24 & 25)*

HALLIDAY THE TIGER

Halliday is the smallest tiger in the rainforest. Although little, Halliday has a mighty roar, which may be heard over a mile away.

Skill Level: Intermediate
Sewing Level: Low-sew

Finished Size: 26 cm

Yarn:

Hobbii Toucan (3.5 oz, 131 yds/100 g, 120 m)

Main Color (MC): Orange (09) for Arms, Tail, Head, Body & Legs - 1 ball

Color A: Black (34) for Ears, Tail, Head, Nose, Body & Paws - 1 ball

Color B: White (01) for Arms, Head, Body & Legs - 1 ball

Materials:

G-6 (4.00 mm) hook

Two 25 mm kawaii sinker safety eyes (alternatively, use 15 mm safety eyes with a 25 mm diameter circle of colored felt behind)

Stuffing

Stitch markers

Yarn needle

Scissors

Black embroidery floss

Orientation Check Points

Read these instructions carefully prior to starting the next round. You may be asked to alter the position of the start of the round before continuing.

EAR (Make 2)

Round 1: With Color A, make a magic ring, 6 sc in ring. (6 sc)

Round 2: Inc in each st around. (12 sc)

Rounds 3-4: *(2 rounds)* Sc in each st around. (12 sc)

Fasten off and weave in end.

ARM (Make 2)

Round 1: With Color B, make a magic ring, 6 sc in ring. (6 sc)

Round 2: Inc in each st around. (12 sc)

Rounds 3-4: *(2 rounds)* Sc in each st around. (12 sc)

Round 5: [Dec] 3 times, sc in each of next 6 sts. (9 sc)

Start to stuff Arm and continue to stuff as you go. Stuff lower 2/3 of Arm only. Change to MC.

Rounds 6-9: *(4 rounds)* Sc in each st around. (9 sc)

Closing Row: Flatten Arm; working through both layers *(to close opening)*, sc in each of next 4 sts. (4 sc)

Fasten off and weave in end. Alternatively, crochet over end when Arm attached to Body. *(image 1)*

TAIL

Round 1: With Color A, make a magic ring, 6 sc in ring. (6 sc)

Round 2: [Inc in next st, sc in each of next 2 sts] 2 times. (8 sc)

Rounds 3-6: *(4 rounds)* Sc in each st around. (8 sc)

Start to stuff Tail and continue to add stuffing as you go. Stuff lower 3/4 of Tail only.

Change to MC.

Rounds 7-9: *(3 rounds)* Sc in each st around. (8 sc)

Change to Color A.

Round 10: Sc in each st around. (8 sc)

Change to MC.

Rounds 11-13: *(3 rounds)* Sc in each st around. (8 sc)

Change to Color A.

Round 14: Sc in each st around. (8 sc)

Change to MC.

Rounds 15-17: *(3 rounds)* Sc in each st around. (8 sc)

Closing Row: Flatten Tail, ch 1; working through both layers *(to close opening)*, sc in each of next 4 sts. (4 sc)

Fasten off and weave in end. Alternatively, crochet over end when Tail attached to Body. *(image 2)*

HEAD

Round 1: With MC, ch 5; inc in 2nd ch from hook, sc in each of next 2 ch, 4 sc in last ch; working on other side of starting ch, sc in each of next 2 ch, inc in last ch. (12 sc)

Round 2: Inc in each of next 2 sts, sc in each of next 2 sts, inc in each of next 4 sts, sc in each of next 2 sts, inc in each of next 2 sts. (20 sc)

Note: In the next round, you will attach the Ears. When attaching each Ear, hold 2 sts of the Ear (you will only work into these 2 sts; the remaining sts are left unworked this round) against the next stitches on the Head with the tip of the Ear pointing down. Work the "attaching" stitches through the Ear (from inside to outside) and the Head together, across both layers.

Round 3: [Sc in next st, inc in next st] 2 times, *(Attach First Ear)* working on First Ear & Head, sc in each of next 2 sts; working on Head only, [sc in next st, inc in next st] 4 times, *(Attach Second Ear)* working on Second Ear & Head, sc in each of next 2 sts; working on Head only, [sc in next st, inc in next st] 2 times. (28 sc) *(images 3 & 4)*

Note: In the next round, you will crochet into the unworked stitches of each Ear. The attaching stitches from the previous round and the slip stitches made in the next round (to prevent gaps) will not be worked into again and are not included in overall stitch count.

Round 4: Sc in each of next 6 sc, sl st across same 2 sts as first attaching st of First Ear; working on First Ear, sc in each of next 10 sts, sl st across same 2 sts as second attaching stitch of First Ear; working on Head, sc in each of next 12 sts, sl st across same 2 sts as first attaching st of Second Ear; working on Second Ear, sc in each of next 10 sts, sl st across same 2 sts as second attaching stitch of Second Ear; working on Head, sc in each of next 6 sts. (44 sc)

Round 5: Sc in each st around *(skipping sl sts from previous round)*. (44 sc)

Round 6: Sc in each of next 6 sts, inc in next st, sc in each of next 8 sts, inc in next st, sc in each of next 12 sts, inc in next st, sc in each of next 8 sts, inc in next st, sc in each of next 6 sts. (48 sc) *(image 5)*

Round 7: [Sc in each of next 5 sts, inc in next st] 8 times. (56 sc)

Rounds 8-9: *(2 rounds)* Sc in each st around. (56 sc)

Orientation Check Point
In the next round, you will start the color changes. The round should start centrally at the back of the Head. If needed, move the start of round forward (by making additional single crochet stitches), or back (by removing single crochet stitches) to allow for this.

Round 10: Sc in each of next 11 sts; change to Color A, sc in each of next 10 sts; change to MC, sc in each of next 15 sts; change to Color A, sc in each of next 10 sts; change to MC, sc in each of next 10 sts. (56 sc)

Round 11: Sc in each of next 25 sts; change to Color B, sc in each of next 7 sts; change to MC, sc in each of next 24 sts. (56 sc)

Round 12: Sc in each of next 12 sts; change to Color A, sc in each of next 9 sts; change to MC, sc in each of next 3 sts; change to Color B, sc in each of next 9 sts; change to MC, sc in each of next 3 sts; change to Color A, sc in each of next 9 sts; change to MC, sc in each of next 11 sts. (56 sc)

Round 13: Sc in each of next 21 sts; change to Color B, sc in each of next 15 sts; change to MC, sc in each of next 20 sts. (56 sc)

Round 14: Sc in each of next 11 sts; change to Color A, sc in each of next 10 sts; change to Color B, sc in each of next 15 sts; change to Color A, sc in each of next 10 sts; change to MC, sc in each of next 10 sts. (56 sc)

Change to Color B. Start to stuff Head.

Round 15: Sc in each st around. (56 sc)

Round 16: [Sc in each of next 5 sts, dec] 8 times. (48 sc)

Round 17: [Sc in each of next 4 sts, dec] 8 times. (40 sc)

Round 18: [Sc in each of next 3 sts, dec] 8 times. (32 sc)

Round 19: [Sc in each of next 2 sts, dec] 8 times. (24 sc)

Orientation Check Point
The next round should start centrally at the back of the Head. Move the start of round by making additional single crochet stitches until you reach the back of the Head.

Change to MC. Do not fasten off.

Face Details

1. Insert safety eyes between Rounds 11 & 12 on either side of the Color B section. *(image 6)*

2. Continue to stuff Head.

3. With Color A, embroider the nose centrally between the Eyes over Rounds 10-12 of the Head in a triangular shape. Make one long horizontal stitch across the top of the nose, then make a vertical stitch down from the bottom of the nose. *(image 7)*

4. With black embroidery floss, embroider eyebrows obliquely over the tops of the safety eyes.

5. With Color B, embroider highlights on the lower outer aspects of the safety eyes. *(image 8)*

6. With Color A, embroider 3 stripes on the top of the Head.

Continue with Body.

BODY

Continue in MC.

Round 20: Sc in each of next 8 sts; change to Color B, sc in each of next 8 sts; change to MC, sc in each of next 8 sts. (24 sc)

Round 21: [Sc in each of next 2 sts, inc in next st] 3 times; change to Color B, [sc in each of next 2 sts, inc in next st] 2 times; change to MC, [sc in each of next 2 sts, inc in next st] 3 times. (32 sc)

Note: In the next round, you will attach the Arms. When attaching each Arm, hold the closing stitches of the Arm against the next stitches on the Body with the decreases of the Arm facing outwards. Work the "attaching" stitches through the Arm and the Body together, across both layers.

Round 22: Sc in each of next 6 sts; *(Attach First Arm)* working on First Arm & Body, sc in each of next 4 sts; working on Body only, sc in each of next 3 sts; change to Color B, sc in each of next 6 sts; change to MC, sc in each of next 3 sts; *(Attach Second Arm)* working on Second Arm & Body, sc in each of next 4 sts; working on Body only, sc in each of next 6 sts. (32 sc) *(images 9 & 10)*

Round 23: [Sc in each of next 3 sts, inc in next st] 8 times. (40 sc)

> **Orientation Check Point**
> The next round should start centrally at the back of the Body. If needed, move the start of round forward (by making additional single crochet stitches), or back (by removing single crochet stitches) to allow for this. If you need to remove stitches that include an increase, make sure you remake the increase so you continue to have the correct stitch count.

Note: Continue in a stripe pattern, alternating Color A and MC each round.

Round 24: (Color A) Sc in each st around. (40 sc)

Round 25: (MC) Sc in each st around. (40 sc)

Round 26: (Color A) Sc in each st around. (40 sc)

Round 27: (MC) Sc in each st around. (40 sc)

Round 28: (Color A) Sc in each st around. (40 sc)

Start stuffing Body.

Note: At the end of Round 29 (next round) and the start of Round 30, you will attach the Tail. When attaching the Tail, hold the closing stitches of the Tail against the next stitches on the Body. Work the "attaching" stitches through the Tail and the Body together, across both layers.

Round 29: (MC) Sc in each st until 2 sts away from center back of Body *(to ensure tail attached at center back of body)*; *(Start to Attach Tail)* working on Tail & Body, sc in each st until end of round. (40)

Round 30: (Color A) *(Continue to Attach Tail)* Working on Tail & Body, sc in each remaining st of Tail *(and matching Body st behind)*; working on Body only, sc in each remaining st around. (40 sc) *(images 11 & 12)*

Round 31: (MC) Sc in each st around. (40 sc)

Round 32: (Color A) Sc in each st around. (40 sc)

Round 33: (MC) [Sc in each of next 3 sts, dec] 8 times. (32 sc)

Note: Discontinue stripe pattern and continue in MC.

Round 34: [Sc in each of next 2 sts, dec] 8 times. (24 sc)

Stuff Body.

Do not fasten off. Continue with Legs.

LEGS

Leg Openings: Join the two central stitches at front of Body to the two central stitches at back of Body with stitch markers *(see photo; the Leg openings on either side of the markers should have 10 sts each)*, sc until you reach first marked central st, [sl st through **front loop** of next central st and **front loop** of opposite central st together, across both layers] 2 times *(these sl sts will not be worked into again and are not included in overall stitch count)*. *(images 13 & 14)*

Do not fasten off. Continue with First Leg.

First Leg

Note: Work into the 10 sts of the first Leg opening only. The next st will be the new start of round.

Round 1: Sc in each of next 10 sts. (10 sc)

Round 2: Sc in each st around. (10 sc)

Change to Color B.

Round 3: Inc in each st around. (20 sc)

Rounds 4-6: *(3 rounds)* Sc in each st around. (20 sc)

Stuff Leg.

Round 7: [Dec] 10 times. (10 sc)

Round 8: [Dec] 5 times. (5 sc)

Fasten off, leaving a long tail for sewing. Use yarn needle to weave yarn tail through front loops of final round and pull to close.

Second Leg

Attach MC to any unworked stitch on second Leg opening of Body.

Rounds 1-8: *(8 rounds)* Repeat Rounds 1-8 of First Leg.

Fasten off, leaving a long tail for sewing. Use yarn needle to weave yarn tail through front loops of final round and pull to close.

1. With Color A, embroider two vertical lines on each foot for the paws. *(image 15)*

Tuva Publishing
www.tuvapublishing.com

Address Merkez Mah. Cavusbasi Cad. No71
Cekmekoy - Istanbul 34782 / Türkiye
Tel +9 0216 642 62 62

Chenille Amigurumi

First Print August 2025

All Global Copyrights Belong to
Tuva Tekstil ve Yayıncılık Ltd.

Content Crochet

Editor in Chief Ayhan DEMİRPEHLİVAN
Project Editor Kader DEMİRPEHLİVAN
Designer Lex Templeton
Technical Editors Megan BARCLAY, Leyla ARAS
Graphic Designers Ömer ALP, Abdullah BAYRAKÇI, Tarık TOKGÖZ, Yunus GÜLDOĞAN
Photography Tuva Publishing

All rights are reserved. No part of this publication may be reproduced, stored in a retrieval system, or transmitted in any form or by any means, electronic, mechanical, photocopying, recording, or otherwise, without prior written consent of the publisher. The copyrights of the designs in this book are protected and may not be used for any commercial purpose.

ISBN 978-605-7834-88-1

The EEA authorised representative is Authorised Rep Compliance Ltd. Ground Floor, 71 Lower Baggot Street, Dublin, DO2 P593, Ireland (www.arccompliance.com)

TuvaPublishing

Acknowledgements:

A big thank you to Kader and the team at TUVA for realizing my dream of publishing this book and to the team at Hobbii for providing all the yarns used to create each design.

To my friend Andreia from @lemonyarncreations, who has been my sounding board throughout this process, obrigado!

Thank you to my amazing team of pattern testers for your time and patience with my terrible spelling and grammar. Thank goodness you didn't have to read my handwriting also. To Coline, Lizzie, Luisa, Alison, Stephanie, Anika, Kim, Megan, Cyn, Lois, Solenn, Jime, Katie, Amelia, Emily, Majoo, Meline, Kiyoko, Elizabeth and Monica, you are all amazing crafters.

Last but not least, thank you to my family for your support and tolerance for all the fluff and stitch markers you continue to find around the house.